The Royal F
in ass
Matthew Gale, J
Michael Edwar

present

The Flags

by Bridget O'Connor

J J	Francis Magee
HOWIE	Jamie Beamish
BRENDAN	Kieran Cunningham
URSULA	Siobhán McSweeney

Director	Greg Hersov
Designer	Laurie Dennett
Lighting	Richard Owen
Sound	Steve Brown
	Claire Windsor
Fights	Renny Krupinski
Production Manager	Eva Walsh
Stage Director	Andrea Laurent
Assistant Stage Director	Marisa Ferguson

Set, Props and Costumes
The Royal Exchange Theatre Company Props and Settings Department

The first performance of this production of *The Flags* was on
Wednesday 8th March 2006 at The Studio, Royal Exchange Theatre, Manchester

The Irish premiere of this production was on Wednesday 27th September 2006
at Andrews Lane Theatre, Dublin

The Writer

Bridget O'Connor

Bridget is the author of two short story collections 'Here Comes John' and 'Tell Her You Love Her', published by Picador. Her short stories have been published in various anthologies and magazines including The Picador Book of Contemporary Irish Short Stories, and have also been translated into French, Italian, German and Serbo-Croat. She has held a number of writing fellowships including Northern Arts Literary Fellow for the Universities of Newcastle and Durham and Writer in Residence at the University of East Anglia and has just completed a Writers Placement at the National Theatre. She won an Arts Council award for radio dramatists 'Write out Loud' and her play, 'Becoming the Rose', was subsequently broadcast on Radio 4. She co-wrote a number of radio plays with her partner Peter Straughan, including 'States of Mind' and 'The Centurions'. Her stage plays include the site-specific (co-written), 'News from the Seventh Floor', (Wils Wilson 2003) set in a Watford Department Store. Her play 'The Lovers' premiered at Live Theatre, Newcastle 2005. Her short film, 'Dead Terry', was produced by the Live Theatre Newcastle in 2005. Her first feature film 'Sixty-Six' (Working Title, co-written) is due to be released in 2006.

The Cast

Francis Magee

Francis has recently finished filming 'Pulling' for the BBC. Theatre credits include 'The Flags', 'Major Barbara' and 'A Midsummer Nights Dream' all at The Royal Exchange Theatre, Manchester; 'The Bench' (BAC), 'Early One Morning' (Bolton Octagon), 'The Bells of Notre Dame' and 'The Best Man' (Croydon Warehouse).

Recent television credits include; 'New Street Law', 'Murphy's Law', 'A Harlot's Progress', 'Trafalgar', 'Battle Surgeon', 'Heartbeat', 'Waking the Dead', 'Slave Trader', 'No Angels' (regular), 'Bad Girls', 'Grease Monkeys', 'The Bill', 'Hustle', 'Red and Blue', 'Family', 'Dead Romantic', 'Born & Bred', 'In deep' and 'Buried'.

Film credits include; 'Sahara', 'Layer Cake', 'Swiss Family Robinson', 'The Calling', 'Don Quixote' and 'Britannic'.

Jamie Beamish

Theatre includes: 'The Tempest' (Corcadorca), 'The Flags' (The Royal Exchange Theatre), 'The Winter's Tale' (UK, Dublin, Spain, New York and China), 'Calico' (West End), 'Much Ado About Nothing' (Peter Hall co.), 'A Midsummer Night's Dream', 'The Two

Gentlemen of Verona' (Ian Charleston Award nomination 2003), 'The Wind in the Willows' (2 seasons), 'High Society' (all at The Open Air Theatre, London), 'The Beauty Queen of Leenane' (York Theatre Royal), 'The Wizard of Oz' (Birmingham Rep), 'The Fair Maid of the West' (Pleasance, London), 'Someone Who'll Watch Over Me' (Eye Theatre), 'Carousel' (Perth Theatre & St. David's Hall Cardiff with the BBC Concert Orchestra), 'Pirates of Penzance' (Open Air Theatre & UK Tour), 'Lord of the Rings', 'The Musical' (Workshop).

TV and Film: 'Atonement' and 'Judge John Deed'.

Jamie was born and bred in Waterford.

Kieran Cunningham

Kieran has previously appeared at The Royal Exchange Theatre in 'Romeo and Juliet' and 'Kes'. Other theatre credits include 'The Quare Fellow'- directed by Kathy Burke (Oxford Stage Company), 'The Lost Warrior' (Duke's Theatre), 'Aladdin' (Liverpool Everyman), 'Forced Upon Us', and 'Working Class Heroes' (Dubbeljoint, Belfast), 'Red Balloon', 'The Birthday Party', and 'Speed-The-Plow'- nominated for Best Actor at the Manchester Evening News Awards (Contact Theatre), 'Spokesong' (Sherman,

Cardiff), 'Midnight Hour (Young Vic, London), Someone Who'll Watch Over Me' (Dukes Lancaster) and 'Grace In America', (Traverse, Edinburgh and Scottish tour). Television credits include 'Shameless', 'Moveable Feasts', 'Shoot to Kill', 'Sometime Never', 'Independent Man', 'Pale Horse' and 'Thieftakers', Film Credits include 'Spanish Gold', 'The Blackburn Files', 'Island', 'The Railway Man', The Jew of Malta', 'Burdalane', 'File on Four', 'The End of Love', 'Divorcing Jack' and 'Catholics'. Kieran was also the voice over on 'The Father Ted Christmas Special'.

Siobhán McSweeney

Irish born Siobhán trained at Central School of Speech and Drama where she was awarded the Carlton Television Bursary given by the Society Of London Theatre's Laurence Olivier Award, 2003. Since graduation her theatre credits include '4.48 psychosis' (Rough Magic Dublin), 'Dark Week' and 'Soap!' (Playgroup,) Girl in 'The Flags' in The Royal Exchange Theatre and Aileen in 'Midden' at The Coliseum in Oldham.

She has just completed filming Ken Loach's latest film 'The Wind That Shakes The Barley' in Ireland.

Siobhán is delighted to be reprising her role in 'The Flags' in her first appearance at Andrews Lane.

Creative Team

Greg Hersov (Director)

Productions for The Royal Exchange Theatre include 'One Flew Over the Cuckoo's Nest', 'The Plough and the Stars', 'Entertaining Mr. Sloane', 'Death of a Salesman', 'Behind Heaven', the Mobile prize-winning 'Woundings', 'The Alchemist', 'A Doll's House', 'The Voysey Inheritance', 'Winding the Ball', 'Blues for Mister Charlie', 'Cockups', 'All My Sons', 'Born Yesterday', 'A Midsummer Night's Dream', 'Cat on a Hot Tin Roof', 'The Crucible', 'She's In Your Hands', 'The Beggar's Opera', an adaptation of Dostoevsky's 'The Idiot', 'Tobaccoland', 'King Lear' with Tom Courtenay, the world premiere of Jim Cartwright's 'Prize Night', Ibsen's 'Ghosts' and 'The Magistrate'. He has worked extensively on productions which have gone on to tour in the Royal Exchange Mobile Theatre including 'Romeo and Juliet', 'A View From the Bridge' (TMA Best Director Award), 'The Comedy of Errors' and 'Little Murders'. He has also directed 'The Road to Mecca', 'Venice Preserved', 'Look Back In Anger', 'Crimes of the Heart' and the world premiere of 'Misfits'. He co-directed 'Mad For It', as well as the original production and revival of 'Animal Crackers' (also seen on tour in the Royal Exchange Mobile

Theatre). He also jointly redirected the show for London's West End and directed 'Look Back In Anger' with Michael Sheen at the Royal National Theatre. Greg also directed the European premiere of Lorraine Hansberry's 'Les Blancs', jointly with Marianne Elliott, 'Uncle Vanya' starring Tom Courtenay, 'The Homecoming' starring Pete Postlethwaite, 'American Buffalo' with Mike McShane, 'The Seagull', 'Ward 6', 'The Playboy of the Western World', 'Major Barbara', 'Volpone' and most recently 'Harvey'.

Laurie Dennett (Designer)

Laurie started his design career in the early sixties within the old three weekly repertory systems as head of design at Manchester's Library Theatre. He first met up with the founding directors of The Royal Exchange Theatre in 1968 when they were running the Century Theatre, which was a theatre that toured the North West in large trailers bringing plays to areas that had never seen theatres. A new director was appointed and the company split; one to carry on to Keswick and the other to form a new company in which Laurie helped to create the Dukes Playhouse in Lancaster. At the same time he joined the 69 Theatre Company as a freelance designer creating the initial structure within the Royal Exchange Great Hall known as the Tent Theatre.

His first season consisted of 'Arms and the Man' and 'Family Reunion', which transferred to the Vaudeville Theatre London. He made the decision to become a freelance designer and found himself working with the director Michael Elliott. This collaboration produced notable productions such as 'The Lady From The Sea' with Vanessa Redgrave, which transferred to the Round House; 'The Dresser' with Tom Courtenay which transferred to the Queens Theatre London and then Broadway where it burned down and had to be resurrected in ten days and 'Moby Dick' which won critical acclaim and a major architectural award, and was Michael's last production before his death.

Laurie had an eight-year break from the theatre and became the director of technical training and design at RADA. He returned to the Exchange in the early nineties to design 'Road' and then was asked to become one of the theatre's associate directors. He is a theatre consultant and worked in collaboration with Terry Farrell on a project for Chester, and more recently the architects Levitt Bernstein on the design of the Royal Exchange Studio Theatre. He is responsible for countless productions at the Exchange over the past thirty years.

His London credits include the opera 'Purtagory' at Sadlers Wells, 'Last of the Red Hot Lovers' at the Criterion Theatre, 'Kingdom of Earth' and 'Ghost of a Perfect Place' at Hampstead Theatre Club. He married the actress Christine Noonan and has five children.

Richard Owen (Lighting)

Richard is the Head of Lighting at The Royal Exchange Theatre , for whom he has lit 'Quids and Dimps', 'On My Birthday', 'Dead Wait', 'Moonshed', 'Across Oka', 'Rafts and Dreams', 'The Happiest Days of Your Life', 'The Rise and Fall of Little Voice', 'Dogboy', 'Mayhem', 'Come Blow Your Horn' and 'Christmas Is Miles Away'. Lighting designs for other companies include 'Brassed Off', 'Bouncers', 'Educating Rita', 'Bedevilled' and 'The Little Mermaid' (Sheffield Crucible), 'Brassed Off' (Sheffield Theatre at the National Theatre), 'Educating Rita' (Plymouth Theatre Royal), 'Brassed Off' (national tour for Centreline Productions), 'Intercourse' and 'Noli Me Tangere (Vincent Dance Theatre), 'Shirley Valentine' and 'After & Before' (Complimentary Productions), 'The Buddy Bolden Experience' (Fittings Multimedia Arts) and 'Flesh 'N' Steel' and 'The Last Freakshow' (Fittings Multimedia Arts in association with The Royal Exchange

Theatre), 'Weeding Cane' (for Weeding Cane in association with the Royal Exchange Theatre), 'In the Shadow of Trees' (for Horse and Bamboo Theatre Company) and 'Christmas Is Miles Away' (The Bush Theatre).

Steve Brown (Sound)

Steve has designed sound around the world, most notably in Tokyo, Madrid, Budapest, Amsterdam and Prague. He has recently returned from Milan where he designed 'Madre Corragio' for the Teatro Strehler in Milan. His extensive theatre credits include, for the Royal Shakespeare Company, 'Richard III' directed by Sam Mendes; Trevor Nunn's 'Measure for Measure' and 'The Blue Angel', 'The Taming of the Shrew', 'Romeo and Juliet', 'The Beaux Stratagem' and 'A Midsummer Night's Dream'. As a resident Sound Engineer for the Royal National Theatre, his numerous credits include 'Sweeney Todd', 'Arcadia', 'The Wind In the Willows' and 'Leave Taking'. Since joining the Royal Exchange Theatre as Head of Sound he has designed over 60 productions including 'Animal Crackers', 'The Road to Mecca', 'Much Ado About Nothing', 'An Experiment With An Airpump', 'Hindle Wakes', 'Peer Gynt', 'Bats', 'Ghosts', 'Snake In Fridge', 'The Taming of the Shrew', 'Les Blancs', 'Uncle Vanya', 'Time and the

Conways', 'The Homecoming', 'A Midsummer Night's Dream', 'American Bufffalo', 'Othello', 'Secret Heart', 'The Seagull', 'Cold Meat Party', 'Hobson's Choice', 'Sherlock Holmes In Trouble', 'Twelfth Night', 'The Playboy of the Western World', 'The Happiest days of Your Life', 'Knives In Hens', 'Great Expectations', 'Six Degrees of Separation', 'Major Barbara', 'A Conversation', 'Volpone', 'Rutherford and Son', 'Anthony and Cleopatra', 'Come Blow Your Horn', 'Sex', 'Chips and Rock 'N' Roll', 'All the Ordinary Angels' and 'Harvey'. He is currently Associate Head of the sound design working group for the Organisation Internationale des Scénografes, Techniciens et Architectes de Théatre,

Claire Windsor (Sound)

Claire has been involved with sound for a number of years. After gaining experience as a live sound and recording engineer, she went on to graduate from LIPA (Liverpool Institute for Performing Arts) in 2004. Since joining the Royal Exchange sound department she has operated a number of shows and co-designed 'London Assurance' and 'Pictures of Clay'. She also designed sound for 'In the Shadow of the Trees', a joint production with Horse and Bamboo Theatre Company.

Renny Krupinski (Fights)

Renny is a British Equity Registered Fight Director, award-winning actor, writer and director. Previous Royal Exchange credits include: 'All the Ordinary Angels', 'Anthony and Cleopatra', 'Volpone', 'Great Expectations', 'The Rise and Fall of Little Voice', 'The Playboy of the Western World', 'Twelfth Night', 'On My Birthday', 'American Buffalo', 'A Midsummer Night's Dream', 'The Homecoming', 'Loot', 'Les Blancs, 'Poor Superman', 'The Moonstone', 'King Lear', 'Prize Night'.

Other fight credits include RSC and most of the theatres in the North West of England and around the country. TV fights include: 'Love Lies Bleeding', 'Blue Murder IV', 'Distant Shores II', 'Beech is Back', 'Coronation Street' (four years and currently), 'The Bill', 'City Central', 'Elidor', 'A&E', 'Emmerdale', 'How We Used to Live', 'Brookside', 'Hollyoaks', 'Peak Practice', and 'The Visitor'.

Television acting credits include 'Beech is Back', 'The Falklands Play', 'City Central', 'Brookside', 'Elidor', 'Just Us', 'Silent Witness', 'A Touch of Frost', and the voice and face of 'Oblivion' at Alton Towers. Royal Exchange appearances include Launcelot Gobbo- 'The Merchant of Venice' and Wemmick- 'Great Expectations' (MEN Award for Best Supporting Actor on its first outing 20 years ago). Other theatre includes Salieri- 'Amadeus' (twice), Capulet- 'Romeo and Juliet', Banquo- 'Macbeth'.

Directing credits include 'Romeo and Juliet', 'Bare', 'A Woman Alone', 'Katie Crowder', 'The Comedy of Errors', 'Arabian Nights', 'Titus Andronicus' and 'Lady Macbeth Rewrites the Rulebook'. Writing credits include 'Bare' (Mobil Playwriting Award), three years on 'The Bill' and many BBC Radio comedies. Last year Renny rode a horse across the Gobi Desert and will soon be directing fights for the Globe season in London, Northern Ballet and Birmingham Royal Ballet.

The Royal Exchange Theatre Company – which was founded in 1968 by Michael Elliott, Casper Wrede and Braham Murray – is the longest-serving group theatre in the country, providing a unique, artistic continuity. In 1976 the Company moved into the Royal Exchange where a purpose built 750-seat theatre in the round was constructed within the former Cotton Exchange Hall.

In 1996, the theatre found itself at the centre of the IRA bomb blast, which devastated Manchester. Two and half years later the Company returned to its home at the Exchange having completed a major rebuild with the aid of a significant Lottery Award. The Theatre re-opened in November 1998 with a completely refurbished 760-seat auditorium and, for the first time in its history a brand new 90-seat Studio Theatre.

The Royal Exchange's aim is to present as rich a spectrum of work as possible, presenting the best in world theatre from the classical to the modern repertoire. The artistic vision of the Company arises from the theatre space itself. The round is three-dimensional like our own lives. The plays look at as wide a spectrum of human experience as possible. A theatre that excludes imaginative other worlds of culture, sexuality and identity is a dead theatre.

New writing forms a central position in our programme and the Studio strengthens these principles by widening our artistic possibilities and providing the imaginative roots for the future. Writers such as Owen McCafferty, Debbie Horsfield, Chloe Moss and Simon Stephens have been nurtured and developed with the best resources available, forming a key part of the Royal Exchange's main repertoire.

In the last year alone, The Theatre has launched three new plays in the Main House and five in the smaller Studio Theatre. 'On The Shore of the Wide World' by Simon Stephens marked our first co-production with the National Theatre, and was recently awarded the Olivier Award for Best New Play.

Centreline Productions

Unit 5a, 3 Long Street, London E2 8HJ

Phone: 0207-739-4952, *fax:* 0207-613-4950
e-mail: jenny@centrelinenet.com

Producers Matthew Gale & Jenny King
Production Assistant: Anne McArthur
Accountant: Jon Catty
Solicitor: Barry Shaw

Matthew Gale (Producer)

For Triumph Productions, Matthew was Production Executive on the following West End productions; 'Collected Stories' with Helen Mirren, 'The Importance of Being Earnest' with Patricia Routledge, 'Hayfever' with Geraldine McEwan, 'Richard III' with Robert Lindsay, 'Prisoner of Second Avenue' with Richard Dreyfus and Marsha Mason, 'A Letter of Resignation' with Edward Fox, 'Life Support' with Alan Bates, the RSC production of 'Herbal Bed', 'When We Are Married' with Dawn French, 'Communicating Doors' with Julia McKenzie, 'Old Times' with Julie Christie, 'Cell Mates' with Rik Mayall and Stephen Fry, 'Electra' with Zoe Wanamaker, 'Talking Heads' with Maggie Smith, 'Uncle Vanya' with Derek Jacobi, 'The Hothouse' with Harold Pinter.

After leaving Triumph Productions, Matthew was General Manager of the Royal National Theatre production of 'Baby Doll' at the Albery Theatre, 'Notre Dame de Paris' at the Dominion Theatre and was production co-ordinator for the Royal National Theatre's US tour of 'Hamlet' starring Simon Russell Beale. He was General Manager on the original London production of 'Rent' at the Shaftesbury Theatre. Matthew also General Managed for David Johnson 'Michael Moore Live at the Roundhouse', 'Footloose' as Consultant for Mark Goucher on tour, General Manager 'Puppetry of the Penis' in Europe and the UK.

Matthew's producing credits include 'Rent' at the Prince of Wales Theatre; 'Auntie & Me' with Alan Davies at Wyndham's Theatre and then the Gaiety Theatre, Dublin. 'Of Mice & Men' with Matthew Kelly and George Costigan at the Savoy which subsequently transferred to the Old Vic starring Joe McGann and Andrew Schofield. Most recently Matthew co-produced 'Elmina's Kitchen' by Kwame Kwei-Armah at The Garrick Theatre, 'The Creeper' starring Ian Richardson at the Playhouse theatre, 'Honour' with Diana Rigg, Martin Jarvis, and Natasha McElhone at Wyndhams Theatre. Matthew was Executive Producer of 'My Name is Rachel Corrie' directed by Alan Rickman at the Playhouse Theatre, Galway Festival and Edinburgh Festival. This autumn Matthew is co-producing 'To Kill A Mockingbird' on a national tour.

Jenny King (Producer)

After spending formative years as Joan Littlewood's assistant at Stratford East, Jenny trained as a theatre designer and won an Arts Council Designer's Bursary to the Library Theatre in Manchester.

Subsequently she designed and directed for four years for companies including: Manchester Youth Theatre, The Haymarket Theatre Company in Basingstoke, Hampshire Youth Theatre, Soho Poly, Buxton Opera Festival and for her own company 'Fit to Bust'.

In 1989 Jenny set up Centreline Productions, her own general management and tour booking agency. In 1995, inspired by her partner Andy Phillips, she started producing; 'The Father' starring Edward Fox and Stephanie Beacham directed by Stuart Burge, co-produced with P W Productions and Adam Kenwright.

In 1997, she co-produced with Pat Moylan, 'Women on the Verge of HRT' by Marie Jones at the Vaudeville Theatre in the West End and on a two year tour. In 1999, she and Pat commissioned 'Women on the Verge, Get a Life!' which toured for nine months in the UK and Ireland. Also in 1999, Jenny co-produced with Kenny Wax and Nick Brooke, Ben Elton's 'Gasping', the first national tour, starring David Haig and subsequently Ian Reddington. In 1999/2000, she co-produced a major 21 week tour of 'Leader of the Pack', a new musical. In 2003 Jenny co-produced 'Auntie & Me' in the West End and in Ireland, and in 2004 she co- produced with Matthew Gale and Bill Kenwright 'Of Mice & Men' starring Matthew Kelly and George Costigan at the Savoy Theatre and subsequently at the Old Vic starring Joe McGann and Andrew Schofield. In 2005, she co-produced with Matthew Gale and Bill Kenwright the National Theatre production of 'Elmina's Kitchen' by Kwame Kwei-Armah at the Garrick Theatre.

In 1996, Jenny formed a company with regional touring venues to produce curriculum related drama. For that company, The Touring Consortium, Jenny has produced: 'Of Mice And Men', directed by Geoff Bullen with Clive Mantle, Lou Hirsh and Harry Towb; 'To Kill A Mockingbird' directed by Geoff Bullen with Richard Johnson; 'The Crucible' directed by Kenny Ireland, with Sean Murray, Alexandra Mathie and Bill Armstrong; 'One Flew Over The Cuckoo's Nest' with Mike McShane, Isla Blair and Danny Webb; 'Anne Frank' directed by Jonathan Church, with David de Keyser, Zena Walker and Lynn Farleigh; 'Four Nights In Knaresborough' directed by Paul Miller, with Nick Moran; 'Hobson's Choice' directed by Jonathan Church, with Tony Britton, Michael Begley, and Katharine Rogers; 'A View From The Bridge' directed by Kenny Ireland, with Robert Gwilym and Sorcha Cusack, 'Taking Sides' by Ronald Harwood, directed by Deborah Bruce and starring Neil Pearson and Julian Glover, 'A Doll's House' directed by Rachel Kavanaugh starring Tara Fitzgerald; 'Dracula' adapted by Bryony Lavery also directed by Rachel Kavanaugh.

In September 2005, a year after losing her partner, Andy Phillips, Jenny formally joined forces with Matthew Gale. This spring they produced 'The Creeper' starring Ian Richardson and directed by Bill Bryden at The Playhouse Theatre, 'Honour' starring Diana Rigg and Martin Jarvis at Wyndham's Theatre, West End and the Birmingham Rep production of 'Romeo and Juliet' on tour also directed by Bill Bryden.

This autumn, they are co-producing 'To Kill a Mockingbird' on tour with West Yorkshire Playhouse and Birmingham Rep.

THEATRE
AndrewsLane

Andrews Lane Theatre,
9-17 St. Andrews Lane, Dublin 2

Tel: (01) 6795720
Email: info@andrewslane.com

Pat Moylan
(Producer & Artistic Director)

Pat Moylan has been Artistic Director of Andrews Lane Theatre for the past 18 years. She has also worked as a freelance producer both in theatre and film and her credits include 'Women on the Verge of HRT' for London's West End and three successful UK tours, a film adaptation of Brendan Behan's book 'Borstal Boy' directed by Peter Sheridan, she co-produced the highly successful play 'Stones in his Pockets' by Marie Jones, for Dublin, the West End and Broadway, 'Thoroughly Modern Millie' for London's West End in 2004 and UK tour in 2005 and 'A Little Bit of Blue' at Andrews Lane Theatre in 2005. Pat recently co-produced 'Tom-Crean: Antarctic Explorer' (winner of the Fringe First Award at the Edinburgh Fringe Festival 2006).

In 1998 Pat Moylan formed Lane Productions one of Ireland's most successful independent theatre production companies. Lane Productions has successfully produced over 50 plays including 'Women on the Verge Get A Life' (Gaiety Theatre, Dublin), 'Alone It Stands' by John Breen which has played in all of the major Irish Theatres, the West End and at the Sydney Opera House, '12 Angry Men' by Reginald Rose (Andrews Lane & Irish National Tour),

'Triple Espresso' (Andrews Lane and National Irish Tour), 'The Blind Fiddler' by Marie Jones, which played at the Belfast Opera House and the Edinburgh Fringe Festival 2004, 'Dinner With Friends' by Donald Margulie, 'Over the River and Through the Woods' by Joe DiPietro and the hugely successful 'I, Keano' which has played to capacity audiences at the Olympia Theatre Dublin and The Lowry, Manchester.

Michael Edwards (Producer)

Michael co-produced 'Twelve Angry Men', directed by Harold Pinter. Other recent credits include a large scale touring production of 'Macbeth' (UK, Calcutta, Delhi, Beijing). He has also produced three tours to major open air Shakespeare Festivals in America, including a production of 'Julius Caesar' in repertory with Houston Ballet's 'Romeo and Juliet' at the 13,000 capacity Woods-Mitchell Pavilion in Houston.

He spent four years on the Board of the English Shakespeare Company, collaborating on several UK touring productions including 'The Comedy of Errors', which travelled on to Jerusalem, Moscow and Kiev.

In 2006, Michael and Carole co-produced Peter Stein's acclaimed production of

'Blackbird' by David Harrower at the Albery Theatre. The play will also be produced off-Broadway at the Manhattan Theater Club in 2007.

Carole Winter (Producer)

Carole spent 10 years at the National Theatre where she produced several small-scale tours, including the first Education tour of 'The Caucasian Chalk Circle' directed by Michael Bogdanov. In 1989 she produced the first Lloyds Bank Theatre Challenge in the Olivier Theatre.

In 1990, she set up the Education Department for the English Shakespeare Company. She built an extensive programme of work that visited schools, colleges, prisons, regional theatres across the UK and international tours to India, Africa, USA, Germany & Beirut. Productions included 'God Say Amen', 'Enemy of the People', 'Macbeth', 'The Tempest', 'The Fantastical Legend of Dr Faust'.

In 1996 she produced her first commercial production, 'Twelve Angry Men', with Michael Edwards and Bristol Old Vic which transferred to the Comedy Theatre in London's West End.

She then headed the development team to raise £1.2m to create the new Soho Theatre and Writers' Centre. From 2002-2005, Carole managed the Artist Liaison Team for Comic Relief covering two Red Nose Days, Sport Relief and Live 8 at Murrayfield.

Carole rejoined forces with Michael Edwards in August 2005 to launch MJE Productions.

Bridget O'Connor
The Flags

faber and faber

First published in 2006
by Faber and Faber Limited
3 Queen Square, London WC1N 3AU

Typeset by Country Setting, Kingsdown, Kent CT14 8ES
Printed in England by Bookmarque, Croydon, Surrey

A CIP record for this book
is available from the British Library

ISBN 978-0-571-23480-6
ISBN 0-571-23480-1

2 4 6 8 10 9 7 5 3 1

Characters

Howie

JJ

Brendan

The Girl

*JJ and Howie – weatherbeaten and dirty –
are lifeguards on the second-worst beach in Ireland.*

*The action takes place over the course of a day
outside their dilapidated hut. Its short tower
is streaked with guano, and dead seagulls are spread
about. Driftwood. Buckets. Surfboards. Rubbish.
Lifeguard paraphernalia. Makeshift weight-training
equipment. An old-fashioned typewriter is set up
on a bucket surrounded by screws of paper.*

A green flag is hanging from a pole.

*The rest of the set comprises a stretch of ugly,
stony beach, ragged clumps of dune grass . . .*

For Peter and Connie-Rose Straughan

Act One

ONE

Lights up on Howie in the tower seat, his rifle by his side. Down below, JJ is sitting up against the hut, typing laboriously on an old-fashioned typewriter. Signs of his industry at the door of the hut and in the screws of paper by his feet.

Howie Read 's it back, so.

JJ No, dude. I'm only after adding one new sentence. You've heard the rest.

Howie Read 's it, go on. I couldn't hear the last time. The fecking seagulls were giving it. I couldn't hear a fecking word. Do and we'll see how it sounds.

JJ pulls up the roller.

JJ Okay, dude. I'd say it's going to sound good.

Howie 'Tis, dude.

JJ 'To the Directorate of Leisure Services.'

Howie Directorate? Who's that?

JJ Brendan.

Howie That's class. It's . . . it's *crawling* but it's good. Can you see himself in his little office in the town hall? (*Mimicking.*) 'Who's this Directorate? . . . Sir Brendan? Why that's . . . myself.' Can you see the big slow smile on his face? It's good, dude, it's good, go on.

JJ 'To the Directorate of Leisure Services . . . Dear Sir or Madam . . . Please find enclosed a joint application for the post of Leisure Operatives . . .'

5

Howie Leisure operatives. That makes us sound like geniuses.

JJ 'As you will see from the enclosed application, Howard Dowd and I . . .'

Howie 'Howard Dowd and I.' That sounds fantastic!

JJ Howard Dowd and I, John-Joseph McKeown, would like to ease the burden of the current vacancies and apply for the posts now sadly available . . .'

Howie Dude, sadly and *tragically* available . . .

JJ 'Sadly and *tragically* . . .' (*He types.*) That's good, dude. 'Available at . . .'

Howie *and* **JJ** Banna . . .

JJ 'Banna Strand. We are experienced in the field as we are currently employed as Leisure Operatives on a . . . popular holiday resort.'

A long pause during which JJ lights a cigarette and we can hear the lonely wind and the seagulls calling.

'Our responsibilities are, chiefly, life saving.' I've put that in capitals. 'Log-keeping. Patrolling.' All of this is in capitals. I'm going to underline 'life saving'. (*He types.*) Dude, I've just underlined 'life saving'.

Howie Car-wreck watching.

JJ 'The care and essential maintenance of life-saving equipment.'

Howie Wind bathing. Shite clearing. Dead animal removal.

JJ 'The provision and maintenance of a first-aid kit.'

Howie What's that?

JJ The plasters.

Howie Oh, right.

JJ 'Pest control.'

Howie Pull!

Howie trains the gun and shoots at a passing flock of seagulls as JJ continues.

JJ 'The monitoring of dangerous currents. Informing the public of said dangerous currents.'

Beat as a dead seagull lands.

This is a new bit. (*He types.*) 'Providing a safe haven' – that's the hut – 'where lost children can be retrieved by their relieved parents.'

JJ continues to type. Pause.

Howie Nobody's been here for weeks, JJ.

JJ I know, dude. I know.

He continues to type. Howie slides down the tower and starts to go into the hut.

Hey?

Howie It's time for my break.

JJ Feck off is it time for yer . . . I'm not doing all the typing and all the fecking application and being eagle-eyed for fecking two while you're – what? Having a snooze?

Howie, defiant, crouches by the hut.

Have you even thought of one?

Howie I have.

JJ waits. Howie thinks.

Ask me the question again.

JJ What are your hobbies and interests?

Howie Er . . . swimming?

JJ You can't put swimming, dude.

Howie Er, surfing?

JJ Ye can't put surfing either.

Howie I don't do anything else.

JJ Lie, dude, make it up.

Howie I might forget it in an interview-type situation. I might crack like under pressure. Can't I have one of yours?

JJ No, dude. You have to do some of the thinking for yourself.

Howie reads from JJ's application.

Howie Foreign travel.

JJ Feck off with that. That's confidential information.

Howie I could have foreign travel.

JJ You haven't been anywhere, dude.

Howie I could have 'Howard Dowd travels widely.' That sounds great.

JJ Hitching from Mrs Simmonds's B&B every day doesn't count as travel, moron-dude.

Howie I've been to my aunt's funeral in Waterford.

JJ It doesn't fecking count, Howie.

Howie I've been to my other aunt's funeral in Skibberrean.

JJ You've got to have been a-broad. I can put foreign travel because I've been somewhere fecking-foreign-abroad. I've been to California, dude. I've spent four fecking years on the West Coast of the world's foremost superpower and you have spent what? An afternoon in Skibber-fecking-rean and a fecking afternoon in Waterford.

Howie Black days.

JJ I'm not interested, Howie-dude.

Howie (*shivers*) There's nothing worse than a funeral.

JJ I don't want to hear your fecking orphan shite now, Howie.

Howie I'm just saying . . .

JJ Well, don't.

Howie takes another peek at the application.

Howie 'Californian cuisine.' What's Californian cuisine?

JJ Tofu. Grilled shite.

Howie You only like Pot Noodles.

JJ I liked tofu then. I still like it. It's very . . . nutritious. Slimming. (*He touches his beer gut, unhappy.*)

I didn't put on like . . . like four fecking stone on tofu.

He shifts his fag to his bottom lip and starts to lift various weights, with difficulty.

I was fit then. I was so . . . This beach in fecking California, dude, where I was like the chief lifeguard . . . Man, I was pumped.

He smokes bitterly. Howie takes another peek at the application.

Howie Say something in Russian, then.

JJ (*Russian babble*) . . . California.

Howie What's that mean?

JJ I wish I'd never left California.

Howie Ye had to come back for your own mammy's funeral.

JJ Yeah . . .

Howie What kind of a dude-cunt would ye be if ye stayed away sunbathing and life-saving Californian girls' lives when your own mammy was having the Hail Marys and the long Our Fathers . . . your own mammy . . .

JJ We're not talking funerals, Howie.

Howie And your poor daddy knee-deep in chickens and your mammy writing every day while you holidayed abroad, dying as she was, having Mass prayers said for yer . . .

JJ I was working. I was a lifeguard on one of the best beaches in California. There was no time for writing letters or . . . or prayer-answering. I had to save lives all the time.

    Pause.

Howie (*muttering*) My own poor mammy. My daddy . . . Ye could have sent Mass cards, JJ. For the funerals.

JJ We're not going to talk funerals, dude.

Howie At least all your relatives aren't dead from assorted cancers. (*Off JJ's look.*) I'm just saying you're the lucky dude. You've still your own daddy putting a roof over your head . . . How old would your old daddy be now?

JJ Eighty-four.

Howie Eighty-four . . . and him still running the McWingy Chicken empire . . .

JJ It's a chicken shed, Howie, and a van.

Howie It's prospects . . . it's more than I have. And ye have your own brother, wee Shaunnessy, dedicated to the chicken-plucking business.

JJ looks at him. Howie picks up a stick and starts to poke the body of a seagull.

It must be nice to have a brother you can do stuff with . . .

He turns the seagull over, absorbed.

JJ (*muttering*) I hate that chicken-stinking fecker wee Shaunnessy . . .

Howie At least ye have someone, JJ. (*Beat, sly.*) And ye still have your admirers.

JJ I have no admirers.

Howie No. (*Beat.*) Well, you have auld Joan . . .

JJ I do not have old Joan . . .

Howie Did you not dance with auld Joan at the Brandon Hotel Christmas last?

JJ For a joke.

Howie And did you not feed her peas?

JJ For a joke . . . Shut up about old Joan.

Howie I'm just saying . . . Feck, I think this thing's still alive.

He looks for something to kill the seagull with. He picks up a flipper.

JJ That's fecking mine!

Howie Oh . . .

He takes off his shoe and starts to whack the seagull.

JJ Feck's . . . sake.

Pause.

Howie I'm just saying you should count your blessings, dude. You have prospects, and family and an old *auld* admirer and feck, it could be worse . . .

JJ indicates the dead seagull and the mess around him.

JJ How? How could it be worse?

Howie Sean Perry and Jimmy Jones could have worn their seat belts.

JJ (*conceding*) True.

Howie (*warningly*) Dude!

JJ instantly stiffens and looks out through his binoculars at the sea.

JJ What is it?

Howie It's gone again.

JJ Can you see it now, dude?

Howie I think . . . it's a dog.

JJ Oh feck.

Howie The tide might take it.

JJ Oh feck, dude. The tide might take it. When did the tide last take anything?

Howie Well . . .

JJ If it's shite or septic it comes to us. If it's like an air-tight box of Marlboro Lights it goes straight to Banna.

Howie (*beat*) You can find good things sometimes.

JJ gives Howie a sharp look. Howie looks straight ahead. Beat. JJ takes the binoculars.

JJ Well, I'm not clearing up dead dog, dude. The seagulls can fecking have it.

Howie We'll have to clear it, JJ. Brendan's coming. We'll have to be shipshape for the inspection. A dead dog looks . . . untidy and doesn't like make a good impression.

They watch the water.

We'll toss for it. Heads.

JJ Okay.

He tosses a coin.

Howie Best out of three.

JJ Feck off, dude.

Howie It might not come in.

JJ Yeah, whatever, dude.

They watch the water.

Howie Ah, shite.

JJ You'll have to go and get it.

Howie Ah, dude.

JJ I did the covering letter.

Howie I can do the covering letter.

JJ Can you spell 'Directorate', Howie?

Howie D – No.

JJ Get off so.

Howie doesn't move. JJ stares at him. Something dark passes between them.

What's the matter, dude? Scared the fat man will get ya?

Howie (*scared*) There is no fat man . . . You're just having a joke. (*Beat.*) Say you're just having a joke, JJ?

JJ You're supposed to maintain vigilance, Howie. That's what lifeguards do. That's the code we live by. You're not supposed to . . . to fecking nap or be like a scaredy-feckin twat around the flags.

JJ lets Howie hang.

Howie (*small*) JJ?

JJ The only fecking fat man round here is you.

Howie breathes out.

Howie Give's a fag so. You gave me a fright there.

JJ writes a number on his packet and hands Howie a smoke. JJ stares out, drawing hard on his fag. We hear the sea, lonely, seagulls calling, the whine of the wind . . . Long pause. Perhaps a wash of sunshine, sudden and unexpected. A mood change.

JJ (*grinning suddenly*) Dude!

Howie (*grinning*) Dude! The tide has turned. I'd say 'the tide' – (*Indicating the sea.*) – has turned.

JJ Has, dude. It'll be different at Banna.

Howie It'll be great!

JJ 'Twill, dude. 'Cos after that it'll be . . . not so great. It'll be chicken-shite breakfast, noon and night. It'll be 'pluck that chicken'. 'No thank you, Shaunnessy dude.' 'Do it!' We'll have to do what the fat chicken-plucking fecker says. We'll have to pluck forty thousand chickens a year.

Howie (*faintly*) Forty thousand . . .

JJ It's a guess, dude. But it'll be worth it, we'll have done it.

Howie We will, dude.

JJ (*warming up*) There'll be no room for petty shite at Banna. You can't be like shooting seagulls whenever you feel like it.

Howie I won't be shooting seagulls at Banna, dude . . .

JJ We'll have to, like, be sharp. We'll have to shape up. We'll have to, like . . . transcend past the old us and, like – I'm including myself here now, mind. I'm guilty of . . . of a certain slovenliness. I've let myself go. I'm not the man I was in California by a long chalk. We'll both have to change our ways.

Howie I'd say you were thinner already, JJ. I'd say you've lost weight since this morning.

JJ I feel thinner, dude.

Howie Definitely. You look all toned.

JJ Thanks, dude.

Howie How many car parks has Banna got now, JJ?

JJ Seven. Not including the caravan park.

Howie Seven fecking car parks not including the fecking caravan park. (*Happily.*) The lifeguards have a gorgeous caravan over at Banna. Like state-of-the-art. We could make salads in it. My mammy, God bless her, before the throat cancer got her, she used to make great salads. Loads of ham. Lettuce and ham, that was my favourite. She always used to wash the lettuce leaves thoroughly. Salad always makes you feel very fit. Just saying the word 'salad' makes you feel skinny. Sal–lad.

JJ Sal–lad. Sal–lad. You're right, dude. We'll have sal–lad and ham then. And fags. We'll have loads of fags. We'll have fags coming out of our ears.

Howie We could get those healthy ones . . . Menthol.

JJ We could, dude.

Howie And we'll be in our flat by then.

JJ (*beat*) Right.

Howie I'll have to give my notice in to Mrs Simmonds so. She'll be heartbroken, but what the feck. We'll be like flatmates. Like having a proper home. Like men in films – you know, like buddies.

JJ Dudes, dude.

Howie Yeah, that's what we'll be. We'll be like lifeguard-dudes, dude.

JJ We will. Skies blue . . .

Howie . . . Waves like skyscrapers. Surfing all day long. Sean and Jimmy, God rest their souls, they had it made. You wouldn't mind dying, like, if it didn't hurt too much, if you'd had a summer in Banna.

JJ They'll be German girls, dude. The Germans love Banna.

Howie We've got German girls at the B&B, they're great . . .

JJ Beauty queens from Tralee. Tits and arse as far as the eye can see.

Howie We could play frisbee with them!

JJ Smoking lovely fags with our cappuccinos, dude. Being helpful with their suntan oil. It's our turn now.

Howie We'll get the application in.

JJ We're ready and available. That's our advantage.

Howie We'll have everything ready. Shipshape for Brendan, sir. I'll get rid of the dead dog so.

JJ Good man!

Howie No more Pot Noodles.

JJ Right. And I won't have a fry-up tomorrow morning and I'll do eighty sit-ups before we go home.

Howie And I'll get a jog in.

JJ And?

Howie Do eighty sit-ups too.

JJ Good man. Get off so. And don't be gassing with Annie at the kiosk.

Howie (*lying*) I won't. Dude, I'd say it was more or less in the bag!

JJ 'Tis.

> *Howie exits. JJ goes into the hut and comes back out mixing a Pot Noodle and wolfing it down. Brendan enters: middle-aged, wearing bottle-ended eye-glasses, a dark suit, carrying his shoes and socks, and sporting a black armband and black tie. He has his hand held up in front of his face.*

Brendan I'm not really here.

JJ Jesus feck. Brendan. Sir.

Brendan Don't worry now . . . don't be getting into a spin. I'm not really here.

JJ I . . . we were just . . .

Brendan You're having a clear up, are ya? No, don't say another word. I have you at a disadvantage. It's a surprise call, so to speak. A social call if you like. This is in no way the official and documented inspection. Don't be minding me at all.

JJ Howie's on his break, Brendan. I have the beach covered. I was just eating a power snack you know. I'm . . . I'm fully alert and operational.

Brendan Have you something to cover my eyes? A shirt or something, John-Joseph? It's hard work keeping the old peep-holes shut. They keep wanting to open and have a good looksy around and if they did and even though I see only smoke and mirrors, the odd spark, without the aul' glasses on you'd be put at a terrible disadvantage over the Castlegrey twins.

JJ Righto. I have er, this here.

He offers Brendan a terrible towel.

Brendan (*rejecting it*) I'll take off me glasses so. 'Twill keep things misty.

He takes off his glasses.

That's grand.

JJ Did you say the twins, Brendan? Are the twins applying?

Brendan That's council business, John-Joseph. I haven't broken confidentiality. Let's say only this. There's a great deal of interest in the post at Banna.

JJ The post. You mean the two posts at Banna, Brendan.

Brendan Do I mean that? I didn't say that.

JJ There's only one post at Banna?

Brendan I didn't say that either. I wouldn't like to talk about council business to a non-official. But if you were to look in my pocket and I was to look in this direction . . .

He shifts to reveal a piece of paper sticking out of his pocket.

JJ 'A pound of rashers. Two pounds of demerara . . .'

Brendan The other pocket.

JJ Oh . . . (*He reads.*) Merged.

Brendan The place runs itself. Sure, there's little need for two lifeguards there so late in the season. It's only our less – (*Beat.*) – populated, more dangerous beaches that we're doubling up these days.

JJ You've only the . . .

Brendan holds up a hand to silence him.

Brendan Not that you're not valued, John-Joseph. Yese are. You have a fierce current out there right enough. I'll say this once, though you know yourself – never underestimate an undertow.

JJ No.

Brendan It looks mild, but is it? There are deep and false waters, John-Joseph, deep and dark. Ely Rock, now, is pure vicious undertow. I'd say even a fine swimmer would have the legs tore out from under them if they didn't mind well. The red flag means something in that vicinity. The two B's, boy: Beware. Be . . . ?

JJ Vigilant . . . I know, Brendan. Er . . . (*Prompting.*) You've only one post at Banna?

Brendan The person who gets that now. It's the best job in Ireland.

JJ 'Tis.

Brendan End to end, boy, it's all tits and arse as far as the eye can see. Many's a time now, stuck in my office on a hot summer day, I'd think of the lifeguards over at Banna sunning themselves . . . listening to the swell of the surf . . . and I'd envy them. I would. For all my rank and privileges as an elected official, a servant of the people, I'd think, and for all I have air-conditioning and my own private secretary, I'd think, and for all I have regular bonuses and my photograph in the paper every other day, God love the press, I'd think about yon lads over at Banna pumping some sweet German tush and I'd envy them giving the old speckie de English.

JJ 'Twas a terrible accident.

Brendan The worst. It could not be any worse.

JJ They were young. Younger than me.

Brendan By a good few years, boy. They were good lads. The best boys in the business. I taught them to swim myself. (*Beat.*) I should have taught them to drive, but there you go. You can't be all things to all men now. Joan is destroyed. She did love those boys.

JJ How is your sister, Brendan?

Brendan She is destroyed. But it's on her account I'm here.

JJ Oh.

Brendan You didn't call her, John-Joseph. You said you'd call her and you didn't call her and now she is destroyed on top of everything else . . . (*He puts up his hand again.*) It is my painful duty to tell you she is destroyed, waiting for you to call. My own big old sister crying her heart out.

JJ I never said I'd call, Brendan.

Brendan You did so.

JJ I never said I'd call, Brendan. I only bumped into her on the path at Mass. I only said good evening and extended my regards to you. I just said, 'Tell Brendan I'll call about the application.'

Brendan 'I'll call' is what she heard. (*Pause.*) She has a new dress made now. She has nowhere to wear the new dress. (*Pause.*) I would not, I think, be breaking brother–sister confidentiality if I was to say, she has always had a yen for you.

JJ She's nearly twice my age, Brendan.

Brendan She's forty only. Maybe forty-four.

JJ I'm only twenty-five myself, Brendan.

Brendan You are not. I know how old you are. I was up at your daddy's last night getting old Joan a bucket of Chicken Wingys, because that is what she is insisting on eating now. To be closer to John-Joseph, that's the kind of shite I'm hearing since the dance at the Brandon Hotel Christmas past. Every night, Chicken Wingys, but only McKeown's Wingys will do. There's no fooling her with a different bucket of chicken. If I was to blindfold her now and test her with an assortment of chicken buckets, she'd pick out McKeown's first time. McKeown's. McKeown's. McKeown's. 'How old is yon John-Joseph?' says I to yon daddy. 'Old enough to fecking know better,' he says, and a great deal more he had to say on the subject of your past behaviour and the tricks you've been up to, womanising for one, making promises that ye don't keep, worrying him out of his mind all those years in California and now back here on one of our less . . . celebrated beaches, in hock to your own daddy, while wee Shaunnessy does the business single-handed and has chicken feathers coming out of his ears and ye wanting to wear the lifeguard's jacket at any cost, even if 'tis here. Ye've a stubborn streak in yer. Am I right?

JJ Yes, Brendan.

Brendan How many seasons have you been here now, mind, John-Joseph?

JJ Five. I've been here five seasons, Brendan.

Brendan Five is what I told him. 'Tis his last season, I assured yon daddy. 'He'd like a chance now at the post in Banna,' is what I said. 'He'd like to go out on top.' Am I right? I am indeed right. I can tell that by picturing your face in my mind's eye. You've had a lick of the lollipop in California, I'd say, and I'd say it's ruined you. I'd say ye'd do anything now to get that post at Banna.

JJ I would, Brendan.

Brendan Anything at all. It's the nearest you'll get to Californ–i-ay again, I'd say. By a long chalk. I've said it before and I'll say it to you now. Are you listening?

JJ I am, Brendan.

Brendan A fella has only one summer, John-Joseph, one summer. There, it's said. (*Pause.*) I would not be now breaking confidentiality if I was to say what your daddy said to me. He said Banna would be a different story now. He could hold his head up if his son had his last post in Banna and then settled steadily down to the old chicken-plucking and debt-paying, and stopped wee Shaunnessy from eating every second Wingy-fecker in sight. There'd be no objection there and only forgiveness in order for sins and crimes committed in the past, including a list of fiancées longer than your arm; the stealing of your own mudder's Post Office book, and various other sundries which are no concern of mine, including your fondness for the horses and the dogs, but which your daddy is fully aware of, but agreed will be forgotten if not forgiven almost in their entirety if you get that post in Banna. Yon Daddy was nodding away.

JJ He has Parkinson's, Brendan.

Brendan (*beat*) Is that right? Parkinson's. That's a dreadful affliction. Is that so? Well, I pity yer both. (*Pause.*) This is just a social call I'm making now. I'll be back for the inspection when you least expect me. Now if you have that application ready, I can take it and save the stamp.

JJ I . . . I have to make some adjustments to it first, Brendan. I'll drop it off at the kiosk so.

Brendan (*beat*) Very good. I'll say ta-ta to you so.

JJ It's good to see you, Brendan.

Brendan stands up and puts on his glasses. He shields his eyes with his hands, preparing to leave.

Brendan The Castlegrey twins are fine swimmers. They have that place shipshape and it was a right shite-hole before. I'd say it was the worst beach in Ireland. Worst than here. Fit as fiddles they are. Fit as fiddles. Shipshape and all in order. Now, if I was to make my surprise inspection there I'd find nothing amiss. And they're good spellers. I've found nothing amiss in their logbooks.

He indicates where we suppose Howie must be walking back from his break.

And yon fellow now, young Howie, is a cracking little swimmer, a proper little dolphin. I'd say he's not out of the game himself. You all have a good crack of the whip at it now. (*He starts to walk away.*) As long as the place is shipshape now, the beach free of wild life, get the blood off the sand, so – I couldn't help but notice it, but as I said, this is just a social call – then you'd all be on an equal footing and may the best man win and none of you will have an advantage over the other or, indeed, any other kind of edge. It's all equal opportunities so.

Pause. He walks away.

Don't let me keep you from your logbooks so.

JJ Oh, right.

JJ steps up to the hut.

Brendan (*as he walks away*) What time will ye be up at the kiosk, John-Joseph?

JJ I don't know yet, I . . . (*Understanding.*) Will you tell old Joan I should be up at the kiosk by three?

Brendan (*offstage*) I will.

JJ goes into the hut and closes the door.

The door of the lifeguard hut opens and sacks of rubbish are thrown out.

We see the bloody wing of a seagull poking erect from a bag. Pause. Then Howie appears from behind the hut breathing heavily through the snorkel mask over his face. He approaches the black bin-liner with the leg of a piebald cow. He attempts to ram the leg into the bag, with eventual success. Disappearing for a moment round the back of the hut, he emerges with the half-wrapped head of a cow. He stands for a moment above the bin-liner, then drops the cow's head onto the sand. Howie talks, but all we hear is a muffled and indistinguishable chatter. Howie turns towards the hut, still talking.

JJ (*offstage*) What?

More muffled chatter from Howie.

JJ (*offstage*) I can't understand a word you're saying.

JJ appears in the doorway. He is holding an old tyre and a Mexican sombrero. He throws them into the heap in front of the hut. Then he sets about trying to dislodge something unseen in the hut.

(*Over his shoulder.*) Take off your mask, Howie.

Howie Huh?

JJ (*raising his voice*) Take off your mask, moron-dude.

Howie takes off his mask.

Howie What?

JJ What do you want? (*Beat.*) You called me.

Howie Oh, right. We've run out of bin-liners, JJ.

JJ (*surveying*) Dig a hole, then.

Howie Who made you fecking boss?

JJ What's in that bag, Howie?

Howie What bag?

JJ You know what bag, Howie.

Howie Oh, that one. Seagulls.

JJ And what's in that bag?

Howie More seagulls.

JJ And who shot all the seagulls, moron-dude?

Howie Don't call me that.

JJ Are you saying I shot the seagulls, Howie?

Howie I'm not saying that.

JJ (*beat*) Who shot the cow?

Howie I was only after putting it out of its misery.

JJ It looked happy enough to me.

Howie It was bellowing, JJ.

JJ It was paddling. It wasn't bellowing. It was – fecking mooing, because that's what cows do.

Howie It was an accident, JJ. I was very sorry after.

JJ Yeah, right. And what about the dog?

Howie (*guiltily*) I'll clear up so.

Howie starts to clear up. JJ sits over a large book.

What yer reading?

JJ The life-saving manual. I'm studying it.

Howie Read 's a bit of it, then. (*Pause.*) Go on. JJ, read 's a bit of your big book.

JJ You wouldn't be able to concentrate, Howie. Your feeble mind would wander.

Howie Would so. I mean, would not.

JJ 'In the event of a fall from a ladder refer to Diagram One. Place the victim on their . . .'

Howie (*approaching*) There's pictures?

JJ Feck off.

Pause, during which Howie dawdles. JJ gives him a narrow look.

I can hear it, dude.

Howie Huh?

JJ I can hear it. I know you're wearing it.

Howie I hear nothing.

JJ (*beat*) I can fecking hear it, Howie.

Howie tilts his head.

Howie You probably have that thing . . . tinny ti-titus my Auntie Ellen had. (*Beat.*) Can you hear . . . like a buzzing?

JJ No . . . it's more of a ticking . . .

JJ makes a sudden grab inside Howie's shirt. He pulls out a watch on a rope and holds on to it, dragging Howie to him by the neck.

You're not to have that, dude. We agreed. Didn't we agree fecking that? Yer to keep it in the fecking box.

Howie Dude, I'm choking.

JJ pushes Howie away. Howie clutches the watch.

I like it, JJ. It has a lovely loud tick – listen.

He holds up the watch.

Tick tick tick tick . . .

JJ It doesn't belong to you, Howie. What if Brendan sees you with it? You'd have some explaining to do then.

Howie You kept that pen.

JJ The pen is different.

Howie And the silver-plated brooch . . . The man's leather wallet . . .

JJ There was no distinguishing marks on those items. What does it say on the back of the watch, Howie?

Howie (*reading*) 'Eternally yours . . . PT.'

JJ That is known as distinguishing marks. That is what would be held up in court and ye'd be marked a criminal for life and fecking kicked off Banna in disgrace. Put it in the box and we'll bury it so.

Howie turns away.

C'mon, dude.

Howie I'll put it back so later. I'll wear it today. It's lovely and warm on me . . . (*He stares at it.*) I wish I had something from me own mammy and me own daddy . . . Just a small thing.

JJ looks uncomfortable.

I'm saying nothing, dude.

JJ You knew the risks, Howie. I didn't persuade yer.

Howie I know, dude. (*Beat.*) I learnt a lesson there right enough, didn't I, dude?

JJ Did yer, dude . . . ?

Howie (*not entirely innocently*) 'A gambler is a right eejit,' that's the lesson I learnt.

JJ Are ye going to put it in the fecking box, Howie?

Howie (*swinging it in front of his face*) No. Tick tick tick tick . . .

JJ makes another grab for it. Howie dances away.

JJ Right!

JJ scrapes a line down the centre of the sand.

Howie What are you doing, JJ?

JJ This is my half and that – (*He indicates.*) – is yours. Fecking stay over there.

JJ moves to the water tank and fills a bucket of water, preparing to wash.

Howie That's . . . (*inspired*) apartheid, JJ.

JJ It is not apart . . . You don't know what you're talking about.

Howie You can be a very petty man sometimes. I mean, for a dude you can be very uncool.

JJ ignores him. He starts to wash himself, sloshing at himself haphazardly with a dirty flannel and a soap on a rope.
Howie walks over to the line.

JJ (*without looking*) Back away from the line, moron-dude.

Howie You've missed a bit. (*Beat.*) Like (*He gestures at JJ's body.*) – everywhere. What you washing for?

JJ (*shifty*) I have a business appointment.

JJ sniffs his armpits. He'll do. He shrugs on his lifeguard jacket – quite a pristine garment.

Howie Feck off, have ye a . . . Since when did ye have . . .?

JJ starts to wet-comb his hair.

(*Pointing.*) You're meeting a girl!

JJ Feck off am I . . .

Howie Ye are. You're washing, and look at yer, all dolled up to the nines. Who is she?

JJ I'm . . . 'Tis no girl.

Howie 'Tis so a girl! Tis!

JJ 'Tis no girl. 'Tis only auld Joan.

Howie stares at him.

Howie You have a date with auld . . . ?

JJ Not a 'date'. It's in the nature of a . . . a favour, that's all it is.

Howie It's . . . (*Amazed.*) That's genius, dude. I'd never have thought of that myself. It's in the bag now. I'd say we were straight in at first place in Banna now. Those Castlegrey boys won't know what hit them. Let me shake your hand.

JJ Nothing's decided.

Howie (*sniggering*) The job's ours.

JJ The job is not ours. We have to pass the inspection first.

Howie A detail.

JJ It is not a detail. It's a pre . . . We have to be up to standard. The logbooks have to be perfect.

Howie indicates a few books lying on a bunch of towels.

Howie I do the logbooks myself. They're great.

JJ He has a chart and he ticks off the boxes. All the boxes have to be ticked.

Howie Brendan's practically your brother-in-law now.

JJ He is not. It's just a one-off occasion. Jest a politeness, a 'Hello, how are ye?' . . .

Howie I'd say you were the coolest dude lifeguard I know. Going through all that auld tea-breath to get us the jobs at Banna. Prepared to smash old Joan's heart too when you move in with me. It's in the bag right enough. You're a fast cruel dude-bastard all right. I feel . . . I feel quite . . . teary.

JJ picks up a logbook and starts to work through the pages.

JJ Will you stop saying it's in the bag. We have to pass the inspection so.

Howie It's in the bag. It's in the bag. We're going to Banna for our summer holidays.

JJ What have you written here, Howie? I can't quite read it.

Howie (*goes over, squints*) That'll be 'ditto'.

JJ Ditto?

Howie As in 'see above'?

JJ And what does that say here, Howie?

Howie That'll be another ditto, JJ. I got sick of making the two little dots.

JJ And what will Brendan think of the two little dots in August, July and – (*He flicks back pages.*) – and all the little dittos in June till we get to – (*He flicks back more pages.*) – the mother of all dittos in fecking May, and reads 'Rain. Red flag. No visitors today'?

Howie He'll think it's the truth at last. Howie Dowd tells no lies!

JJ He'll think that's a fine way to spend public sector wages on two lifeguards who can only manage a pair of fecking little dots between them.

Howie You said to keep it short.

JJ Succinct. I said to keep it succinct . . . I said to write in it every fecking day. You said you were writing it every fecking day. Ah what's the fecking point? I should have fecking known I couldn't fecking trust a wee shite like Stinky-Shitey Howie Dowd.

Howie Don't be calling me Stinky-Shitey. Nobody calls Howard Dowd Stinky-Shitey any more.

JJ With his 'Oh let me, JJ, oh please, JJ.' I'm too soft in the head. I'm too . . . kind, that's my trouble. That's what old Joan says I am, any road. According to her I'm all fecking heart.

Howie mumbles indistinct swear words.

What's that?

Howie I said it's fine weather we're having.

JJ That is not what you said.

Howie I said Mary Walshe doesn't think you're all heart.

JJ I was never with Mary Walshe. Apart from that one time.

Howie Patricia Quinn doesn't think you're all heart.

JJ I was never with Patricia Quinn . . . It was her twin sister . . . I'm not listening to your blather now. I've work to do.

He starts to write in the book. Beat.

Howie Una Flaherty up at Flaherty's Hotel . . .

JJ Now I was never with Una Flaherty from Flaherty's fecking Hotel for feck's sake.

Howie I know. She just thinks you're a cunt. She thinks you're fat, too. No, those weren't her words, her words were, 'John-Joseph used to be a fit bit before he fecked off to America but now he is just a' – hold on a second now, I think I'm quoting her correctly – 'a fat and useless cunt.'

JJ Is that right?

Howie I'm only quoting what's said. Annie at the kiosk says no girl would have you now. She said ye drive girls mental with yer lies. Now you have to go for the proper auld un's. Like Joan. Except you have to fecking marry them now instead of just fecking breaking their hearts and making them have fecking abortions in England. Joan will have you on a tight leash. Her auld Pekinese dog will have more leash than you. Her auld Pekinese dog has more balls than you.

JJ I'm sad you said that now. I'm awful sad. Especially as I have something in my pocket now. A surprise it was, but no matter. (*He pats his pocket.*)

Howie What's that?

JJ It's just a great pity. No, don't bother now. The moment's gone. (*He takes a piece of paper from his jacket.*) There have been things said that perhaps should not have been said. Insults traded.

Howie What do you have there?

JJ No, the moment's gone now. I'll apply to Banna so with Tommy Frank.

Howie The lice man!

JJ That problem has been dealt with. He is no longer hatching.

Howie You're joking me now. You've the applications sent off, I know it.

JJ My friend-dude, how I wish that was true.

Pause.

Howie Ah Jesus, you had me going there. You're a bad fella. A right bad fella all right.

JJ You'll have to write a letter yourself now, Howie, listing your own achievements, hobbies and interests.

Howie C'mon now, JJ, the joke's over. 'Tis all done.

JJ I have work to do, Howie. I have my own future to attend to. I have descriptions to write for the logbooks. Vivid descriptions. Brendan could be here at any hour and I have to take the rubbish to the dump.

Howie I'll do it.

JJ I have to sweep out the hut.

Howie Consider it done.

JJ I have the flags to change.

Howie I'll do it.

JJ And I have a swim to take.

Howie A swim? You haven't been for a swim for . . . You hate the water.

JJ I just hate this water, Howie. Someone has to test the tides. For authentic description purposes.

Howie But it's . . . it's all wet.

JJ takes out a sheet of paper and pretends to tear it.

Howie I'll do it.

JJ All the way to the rock now.

Howie reaches for a wet-suit.

Just the trunks, Howie.

33

Howie But . . .

JJ 'Please describe how you could best contribute to . . .'

Howie slips off his clothes and is revealed, very pale and sickly, in his trunks. Only his face and hands are dark brown. JJ holds his hand out and Howie gives him the watch. Howie exits to the right, grumbling.

And don't swallow anything.

A beat. Then JJ turns his collar up, takes a look in the shaving mirror, and slopes off.

THREE

A dishevelled Girl in a greatcoat and wellington boots, carrying a rucksack and with a stem of seaweed in her long hair, appears. She sits and starts to examine the stones, instantly absorbed. Howie emerges from his swim. He is drenched and exhausted and staggers about for a moment before collapsing to his knees and hacking mightily.

Howie Jesus fuck. Jesus H feck and fuck. That was unbelievably fecking horrible.

He tastes something vile in his mouth and spits.

Ah God, I am never going in there again. I am . . .

He lies back on the stones panting, then scrabbles madly inside his trunks, standing and flinging something awful away.

Fecking fuckity feck fuck! I am never going in there again. I am never . . .

He spots the Girl and starts. He immediately puffs himself up. He starts to perform a number of exercises, breathing flashily. The Girl is in her own world, still sorting the stones.

Brrr. That was fantastic altogether. Gets the old blood going any road, eh?

She ignores him. She holds a stone up to the light and seems fascinated by it.

I said it gets the old blood pumping . . . Are you going in yourself? . . . I swam about eight miles then, give or take. Me heart's pounding. The water's lovely. Like silk. Well, like petrol any road. Takes a bit of getting used to . . . I said it takes a bit of getting used to . . . Are you here on yer holidays, like? Hello? I'm being civil to yer . . .

Something tremendous occurs to him.

Ah, ah, I see. You're, um, I see, uh . . . You're . . . er . . . hold on a second now. Hold on now, I have it! (*Long pause. Deep breath. Loudly.*) Speckens de deutsch?

The Girl looks around as though she can just hear something, then goes back to sorting stones.

No. No. It's specken de English! She must think I'm like an eejit. (*Very loudly.*) Specken de anglaise? This is not Banna. This – (*Indicating.*) – is not Banna. But you are very welcome at our beach. Uh. Me Lifeguard Howie. Howie. (*Pause.*) Do you know Hargar and Uti? Hargar and Uti? They're German girls. German. Staying at Mrs Simmonds' B&B. From Hamburg, many miles from here. Hamburg? Where the Germans live.

The Girl looks up blankly and holds up a small white stone.

Girl This . . . this is my favourite one.

Howie Hargar's my favourite. Real friendly like. She gives me her black pudding every morning now, once I told her what was in it . . . How's that?

35

Girl It's a very pure white. See? Perfectly round. Beautiful. This one here has a little chip on the side, like a fingerprint. Can you see? Like someone's leant on it millions and millions of years ago. But this one – (*From her pocket.*) can you see this one? 'Tis precious. A fossil . . . Do you see the face?

Howie I see nothing . . .

Girl (*pointing*) That's a dead thing. That's the wee eye and that's the line of the mouth . . . When you die you sink into rock. You imprint yourself. That's what I want . . .

Howie Eh . . . ?

Girl 'Tis the jewel he gave me.

Howie Who?

Girl My fiancé. (*Her face crumples.*)

Howie Don't be getting upset now. Never mind the dead thing . . . Where's this fiancé of yours?

The Girl points to the sea.

Howie Swimming?

Girl America.

Howie Eh?

Girl He said 'twas as good as a diamond. That's what diamonds are. They're dust. 'Tis the sea that turns them sparkly. 'Twas one of the first things he said to me.

Howie What . . . who?

Girl Are ye thick? My fiancé. He said 'Do you want to dance?' Of all the girls, he asked me. 'Do you want to dance?' (*Very solemnly.*) I said, I can remember it like yesterday, I said, I said, 'I do.'

Howie Have you had a knock on the head, is that it?

36

Girl (*fast*) He said, 'Would you like to see a diamond?'
I said, 'I would.' He said, 'Get in the car so.' I did. He
said, 'Step down here to this wee beach. 'Tis not far, 'tis
not dark.' 'Twas. 'Twas. He said, 'Wait, wait.' And he
had his arm round me, and the moon sailed out and lit
the stones and they were, they were like diamonds. It was
not a lie. I remember it like yesterday. We lay down.
There were stars above me, diamonds below. His mouth
on me. He said, could he? I said no. He said, 'Let me.'
I said no. He said, 'We'll marry so.' I said, 'Will we?' He
said yes. Of course. He said, 'God Almighty, of course!'

Howie That's great.

Girl Daddy says he's to America. I said, 'I'll wait so.' He
said, 'You know what you are?' I said, 'I do, Daddy.' He
said, 'And do you know what you're not?' He said,
'You're no fecking daughter of mine.' I said, I said,
'Daddy, I am. I am.' I said, 'Love is not a disgrace. Love
is worth waiting for . . . 'Tis, Daddy,' I said. 'I'll wait.
He'll come for me. He promised.' (*Searching.*) This was
where we lay together. Or . . . or it was here . . . I can't
remember . . . This might have been the place . . .

Howie Are you here on your holidays?

Girl Where are the diamonds? I have only five of the
white ones and I've been searching all night. What am
I going to do now? Oh God. What am I going to do?

Howie Don't be getting upset. They're only rocks like.
We've fecking loads of them.

Girl Oh God, what am I to do? I can't wait any longer.
I'm so tired . . . (*She starts to bang her head. Muttering.*)
The white one . . . the white one . . .

Howie Look it! I'm helping ye. Don't be getting upset.

He holds up a stone.

I have one!

The Girl stares at him.

Girl (*fury*) That is not a fecking white one!

Howie 'Tis . . . 'tis . . . It just needs a little rinsing.

He polishes a stone on his shorts.

To bring up the whiteseyness. Look! Look! This one's gorgeous! I'd say it was the most beautiful rock I've ever seen. I'd say, once I got rid of . . . of the seagull blood, like . . . There!

Girl (*instantly calm*) More. More.

She holds out her hands. Howie sits down and scoops a load of stones towards him and starts cleaning them with spit. The Girl examines each stone with great particularity and starts making two piles.

Do you think he'd like this one?

Howie Yes.

Girl Pretend to be him, so. Which one do you like?

He chooses. She holds up two more.

This one . . . or this one?

Howie (*choosing*) That one.

Girl This one . . . or this one?

Howie chooses.

Are you still pretending to be him?

Howie No. I don't want to.

Girl Pretend to be him.

Howie All right.

Girl Do you love me?

Howie Yes.

Girl I love you.

Howie beams. She kisses him.

Howie Feck's sake . . . that's great. Will I see ye again?

Girl Would you turn your back. I have to change now.

Howie You're going in? Really?

Girl I have no swimming costume.

Howie (*blushing*) Oh.

Girl You won't look?

Howie You're going in . . . in the nudey?

Girl You won't look, will you? (*Urgent.*) Promise you won't look.

Howie Promise. Not a peep.

She nods. Howie turns his back. He puts his hands over his eyes.

Peepo! Only kidding.

The Girl takes off her coat revealing a long white gown. She takes out a wedding veil from her rucksack and puts it on. She picks up a long strand of seaweed and holds it. She puts her rucksack on, having to steady herself against its weight.

Well, as the lifeguard, I'll tell you now, you're to paddle only. Stay away from Ely Rock. There's a terrible savage tide there. It has terrible suction power.

Girl Ely's Rock. Straight ahead?

Howie It'll take the legs out from under ya. Right out from under ya.

Girl Goodbye.

Howie Ta ta so. It was lovely chatting to you. I won't look so. You're away, are you? I'd say you were on your way now are you? Shall I see yous later . . .

Girl (*distantly*) Yes. I'm away now.

She exits.

Howie (*calling after her still with his eyes closed*) It's a date so. It's a date. It's been great chatting to you. I haven't had a chat like that in ages now. Not since my sister Majella died of leukaemia and I used to keep her company on her hospital bed. We used to have great chats then. (*Pause.*) Did I tell you I was an orphan, did I mention that?

JJ enters and heads immediately to a bucket. Takes a bottle of mouthwash and gargles with it thoroughly. He sees Howie standing in a dream.

Love's brilliant, isn't it, JJ?

JJ spits out the mouthwash.

How was auld Joan?

JJ Do I have to do fecking everything? You should be clearing up the place. Fecking move.

JJ, tidying, starts to back Howie towards the tower.

Howie I'm in love, JJ.

JJ Well, it's not reciprocated, gay-dude.

Howie Huh?

JJ I said you're on your own, creepy-dude, with your sex-talk. Now feck off up there and write the tides. Write them good now or I'll come and bludgeon yer.

Howie climbs a few steps. JJ picks up a hammer from a bucket and starts to straighten the LIFEGUARD *sign.*

JJ And feck off with yer dittos.

Howie I was on a date too, JJ.

JJ (*warning*) Dude . . .

Howie My head's spinning like a top from her gibberish. (*Happily.*) I didn't understand a fecking word she said.

JJ takes a look at him.

JJ You drank sea water. Didn't I say not to swallow the . . . but you couldn't keep yer fecking gob shut could ya? Now you're septic. (*Muttering.*) Fecking girl. (*Gesturing around.*) What girl, dude?

Howie She was here, JJ, she was, I swear. There was all this . . . there was hair and . . . and we . . . we talked . . . about geology and stuff and rocks.

JJ Feck off with yer geology.

Howie She kissed me.

JJ Now I know you're hallucinating. Who'd kiss you?

Howie's confidence starts to drain. He scans the beach with his binoculars. To the right . . .

Howie (*less certain*) She was here, JJ . . . I swear . . .

JJ Yeah . . .

Howie scans to the left.

Howie (*beat*) . . . There's something in the sea, JJ.

JJ Huh?

Howie I think . . . I think there's something in the sea.

JJ looks through his binoculars.

JJ It'll be that dead dog, dude.

They both look out to sea through their binoculars. Long beat. JJ drops the hammer. He mouths 'Feck.'

Quick black.

FOUR

JJ is standing over the unconscious blood-soaked Girl, looking shocked. Then, as though waking, he gives her crap mouth-to-mouth. The Girl, who is still wearing her wedding gown and veil, is lying on a stretcher. Howie is walking about agitated. They're all soaking wet.

Howie She's dead. She's fecking dead. Feck. Fuck. Is she dead? Oh fuck me, feck fucking me.

JJ (*between breaths*) Get the . . .

Howie What? What? Jesus . . .

JJ Get the fecking book.

Howie (*beat*) This is no time to . . . to *read*, JJ, Jesus . . .

JJ The . . . fecking . . . life-saving . . . manual . . .

Howie Jesus . . . Yes . . . feck, where is it?

Howie steps up into the hut. He rummages.

Hey, it's all tidied. I can't find a fecking . . . JJ, I found . . . I've got it. I've got it.

He tumbles out carrying a large first-aid tin and the book. He falls flat on his face.

JJ Cunt.

Howie Hey . . .

JJ She's not breathing . . .

JJ gets on the Girl's chest, thumping her heart randomly.

Howie Is that . . . Are you doing that right? That doesn't look right, JJ.

JJ I can't quite . . . I can't quite remember . . . Page . . .

Howie flips pages.

Howie Yes . . . yes . . . hold on . . . life-saving, um recovery positions, burns, no . . .

JJ Howie!

Howie Here it is . . . Drowning . . . drowning . . . ponds, lakes, seas . . . page 109 . . .

Howie finds the page and turns the book over a few times.

JJ I think . . . you . . . you do . . .

Howie Your hands are all wrong. JJ . . . Your hands should be as in Diagram E, like this.

He gestures. JJ copies him.

Other way. No, no, my left. Mine . . . The one with the freckle on it . . . I'll do it. I'll do it. You read.

They swap places. JJ begins to pace with the book.

JJ And a one-two-three-four. And a one-two-three-four . . .

Howie You're putting me off . . .

JJ And a one-two-three-four. And a one-two-three-four . . .

Howie I didn't do that when you were . . . You're fecking . . .

JJ Aaand a one-two-three-four . . .

Howie You're fecking putting me off. Feck off, man . . .

He tries to swat JJ.

JJ It's the rhythm, moron-dude . . . Press. Aaaand a one-two-three . . . Then . . . (*He turns the page.*) Pages 110 to 115 are missing. Howie, pages 110 to . . . Did you? Pages . . . Did you wipe your arse with pages 110 to . . . Howie? Did you . . . ?

Howie 'S okay. I remember it now.

JJ What are you fecking about for? Save her!

Howie I just remember this bit. You count. You go one-two-three-four-*five* . . . We had to practise on this dummy at the pool . . . Margaret. Brendan took her out of a box. (*Pause.*) It's different with a dummy, JJ.

JJ Get . . . Save her!

Howie You . . . you do something first. You . . . you . . . tilt or . . .

He picks up the Girl's wrist. It falls limply down.

Oh Jesus . . . she's freezing . . .

JJ She's dead. You've killed her, murdered her with your pissing about.

Howie (*crying*) You're the chief lifeguard of fecking California! You save her.

JJ turns towards the hut, biting his knuckle.

Or you . . . you, you, cover the nose first, no . . . you . . . I can't think . . . clear the airways. It was easy with Margaret. You just had to . . . kind of pound her . . . (*He deepens his voice*) 'You're on a beach. The victim is not breathing. You focus your . . .' Oh Jesus, she's freezing cold . . . I'm sorry, lady . . . I'm so sorry . . .

Suddenly JJ goes into the hut and wrenches something, with effort, from inside. He comes out with a large box. He opens the box and out comes a female life-saving dummy.

I wondered what was in that.

They swap places. Howie 'resuscitates' the dummy, JJ resuscitates the corpse.

You clear the airways.

44

JJ copies the movements.

JJ Uh . . . lasagne. Fuck me.

He pulls out a large piece of seaweed from the Girl's mouth.

Howie Gently press the nostrils together. Take a large breath and . . . one-two-three. Listen to the mouth.

They both listen to the mouths.

And repeat. One-two-three. Listen to the mouth.

They both listen to the mouths.

And repeat. One-two-three. Listen to the mouth.

They both listen to the mouths.

I think . . . I think she's . . . she's breathing!

They both look at the inflated dummy.

JJ Thank feck . . .

They both look at the corpse.

Howie *and* **JJ** Oh. (*Long pause.*) Feck.

Blackout.

End of Act One.

Act Two

ONE

The lights rise as Howie and JJ, wearing their lifeguard jackets, enter carrying spades. JJ lights a cigarette.

Howie We should have said a few words.

JJ There wasn't time, Howie.

Howie We should have sung something, then. That's what you do at funerals. I think Grace . . . I think Grace would have liked a song.

JJ (*beat*) How do you know her name's Grace?

Howie I don't. She just . . . she just looked like a Grace. I tried out other names but . . . they didn't suit her. I tried out Gráinne.

JJ I'm not interested, Howie. Give me the rucksack so and we'll bury that.

He hides the rucksack.

Howie . . . And Gretta. That doesn't suit her. Gloria, Gina, Jolene, Geraldine . . .

JJ Fecking get a hold of yourself.

Howie Say Geraldine. Maybe that suits her better. Say Geraldine, JJ.

JJ pulls out the looting box.

JJ Put her wee bits and bobs in here so.

Howie takes a wristwatch and a ring from his pockets. JJ takes a gold chain from his. Howie pulls out the fossil necklace from around his neck.

You can keep the dead thing.

Howie nods. JJ puts the looting box in the hut. Howie starts to lower the flag.

JJ What are you doing? Dude?

Howie I'm paying my last respects.

JJ We haven't time for that now. You can't just lower the fecking flag when you feel like it, Howie-dude. Fecking put it up again.

Howie ties the flag at half-mast. JJ smokes.

She was probably dead already.

Howie She was breathing when I turned her over. In the water.

Pause.

JJ You didn't say that before.

Howie She made a sound like . . . shhhhh. Sort of like . . . It was her death rattle.

JJ Bollocks was it her death rattle.

Howie It was. I also heard a kind of . . . gasp.

JJ Get to feck.

Howie I did. It was the same noise my Auntie Betty made when she died.

JJ I don't want to hear your orphan shite now, Howie . . .

Howie And my Auntie Lucy . . .

JJ Or your Auntie Lucy . . . God rest her.

Howie All . . . lonely, like the wind in a shell.

He starts to cry, shoulders shaking.

JJ Oh feck it, Howie. What if Brendan came now? How will I explain you crying and fecking . . . carrying on?

47

And the flag half-cocked like it is . . . What kind of impression will that make?

Howie I'd say me crying and the half-cocked flag is . . . is the least, the least . . . We're not going to make 'a great impression', dude. There's a dead girl. We killed her.

JJ We did not.

Howie Okay, you did. You killed her.

JJ I . . . ye what?

Howie It took you long enough to follow me in, didn't it?

JJ I thought it was the fecking dead dog . . .

Howie I'd been under five times already dragging her up from the bottom and when I fecking surface in the fecking boiling surf you're only at your knees oohing about the cold.

JJ You were wet already, Howie. You had the advantage.

Howie We're lifeguards. We're supposed to save people, JJ. We're . . . we're not supposed to . . . to worry about a few fecking cold splashes.

JJ turns away, stung. Pause.

JJ She must have been under there for . . . well, it was a long time any road. Whoever she is, she wanted to die. It's obvious. For all we know she might have taken pills as well or something . . .

Howie She was having a paddle only. She had everything to live for. We had a date for later . . . We did. She liked me . . .

JJ What was she wearing, Howie?

Howie 'Twas a beautiful white dress.

JJ A fecking wedding dress. And what did she have round her neck?

Howie The dead thing.

JJ Apart from the dead thing?

Howie A bag.

JJ What did she have in her bag, Howie?

Howie Rocks. Stones and rocks.

JJ I rest me fecking case.

Howie No . . . no, see she just collected them because . . . because they're as . . . as beautiful as diamonds. I helped her . . .

JJ (*beat*) You helped the dead girl put rocks in her rucksack?

Howie Yes. No. Yes. She said the white ones were the perfect ones . . . I . . . It . . . it wasn't like that, she liked me, she . . .

Coming to a sad decision, Howie takes a skateboard from the hut and prepares to leave.

JJ Where you going, dude?

Howie I don't think . . . I don't think we're very good at saving people, JJ . . .

Howie's walking. JJ catches up with him.

JJ Feck off with that talk, Howie . . . Howie . . . Stop, dude. Stop. Just listen for a sec. Listen. They don't let you be lifeguards if people go drowning all the time . . .

Howie shrugs him off. JJ walks close to him.

(*Smiling, tight.*) One second now. (*Beat.*) What am I good at that you're not?

Howie Huh?

JJ That's right. Thinking. Thinking, dude. Now just give me a minute here . . . to think. Another minute or so won't hurt, will it?

Howie I s'pose.

JJ Okay. Okay. (*Pointing.*) See that flag over there?

Howie Yes.

JJ And do you see that flag way over there? (*He points in the other direction.*)

Howie Yeah.

JJ Now. Now . . . do you want to spend the rest of the summer . . . the rest of the fecking season, every fecking day, toiling between those two flags, hoping you trip on a rock so you can spend some of it completely unconscious? Yes or no . . .

Howie That's not the . . .

JJ Yes or no. One word, dude. One word.

Howie I . . .

JJ One word.

Howie No.

JJ Because if you answer yes, then you just go right ahead and tell Annie at the kiosk and the fecking gardaí and ye go straight to prison for giving rocks to a suicidal girl and ruin our chance of eating ham salads at Banna and having our own flat together at last, like buddy-dudes . . .

Howie I . . . I . . . You're confusing me, JJ . . .

JJ You did her a favour. She's with him now, her fiancé, maybe not in body, but in spirit. That's what she wanted. (*Pause.*) C'mon, dude . . .

Howie stops. JJ puts his arm round him.

Have a sit down. Ye've had a nasty shock all right. C'mon now. You're a good little fella, c'mon now. Will I get your blankie?

Howie nods. JJ presses Howie down onto the sand. He pulls Howie's red towel blankie around him. He puts his arm round him, one eye on the horizon, restless. Howie quietens, comforted.

Howie (*small*) JJ, what if he finds out?

JJ He won't. (*Pause.*) Dude, we haven't done anything wrong.

Howie looks at him. Pause.

Howie Didn't we bury two people under the flags, JJ, not including Grace?

JJ Yes, we did, yes. But . . . we didn't . . . we didn't kill them, Howie. They drowned . . . accidentally.

Howie We didn't save them . . .

JJ Technically, no. No. But . . . we tried. We tried to save them. Perhaps . . . perhaps we weren't as . . . as vigilant and aware as we should have been, but lessons were learnt. We're better Leisure Operatives today because of them. Aren't we always in the watch tower, watching? And aren't we on patrol all the fecking time? Well, most of the time. Some people . . . they don't want to be saved.

Pause.

Howie (*small*) The fat man wanted to be saved.

JJ Okay, yes, yes, he did. But he was . . . he was fecking huge . . .

Howie The aul' tramp lady . . .

JJ Well . . . yes, she did, too. But you said yerself, didn't you say yourself, you thought it was a seagull cawing . . . listen, they sound exactly the same.

A seagull squawks.

Can you tell the difference between that now and a drowning aul' tramp lady? (*Beat.*) She shouldn't have gone into the water if she couldn't swim properly. The fat man, well, what did the fat man have in his togs, Howie-dude?

Howie Sweeties. He had sweeties in his togs.

JJ That's right, sweeties. He shouldn't have eaten all those sweeties if he wanted saving one day . . . There's deep and false waters by Ely Rock, now everybody knows that. They had no business being here drowning. They should have been splashing and jumping the waves at Banna. Didn't we have the red flags up?

Howie shakes his head . . . They didn't.

JJ Oh. Well, we did this time, and it made no difference so.

Howie I feel terrible, JJ.

JJ I know, dude. I know. I don't feel so good myself. But it'll pass. You know what . . . what we'll do. Me and yous, Howie, we'll go out for a drink. Will wes? Remember last year now? We'll go to Flaherty's.

Howie I . . . I wish this was over, JJ. I wish it was like the . . . day after tomorrow.

JJ Just . . . just think about something nice, Howie. Think about the flat.

Howie mumbles indistinctly.

JJ What's that?

Howie There isn't going to be a flat, is there, JJ?

JJ Of course there is, dude. (*Beat.*) Of course there's going to be a flat. What makes you say there isn't going to be a flat?

Howie Annie at the kiosk . . .

JJ Oh, feck Annie at the kiosk . . .

Howie She says it doesn't take five years to save up for a deposit, JJ.

JJ It's taken . . . hang on a second . . .

He looks through the binoculars briefly, playing for time.

It's taken that long because, Howie, because, because, Howie, the flat we live in, Howie, right, you and I, it can't be just any old flat. It has to be . . . the perfect flat. And the perfect flat requires thought. Careful careful planning. I've got it all up here. (*He taps his forehead.*) All laid out.

Howie Yeah.

JJ All laid out, Howie. Every detail. (*Pause.*) You don't believe me?

Howie I didn't say that.

JJ I'll prove it to you.

He takes a stick and starts to draw on the sand.

The door to our flat. Now you can have it any colour you want, but I favour red. You walk in through our red door and ye nearly suffocate because the heating's on so high. Can ye see it? It's all toasty and warm. (*He mimes.*) Here's the lounge, right, Howie-dude. And these. These feckers are our chairs. Ye flick a button and the chairs go right back. And that . . . that is our television like a fecking cinema. And on either side of that is, like . . .

Howie Leopards. Black leopards.

JJ I was going to say mini-fridges but . . . black leopards it is. (*Beat.*) Feck it, we'll have the fridges too. And here. Here is our fecking spiral staircase – (*He squiggles on the sand.*) – and up, up past the floor we use for having wild parties on, are our bedrooms. Our bedrooms, Howie. Think right: chrome and leather, Howie. Chrome and leather. Don't think Mrs Simmonds kicking you out to the couch because she wants to rent ye own room to fecking toilet-cleaner salesmen, think king-size bed. Think jacuzzi. Think power-shower. Think dudes, dude.

Howie It looks . . .

JJ holds up a finger and wags it.

JJ Sshh. I haven't finished yet. Ye press a button and the doors swing open like automatically and what do ye see?

Howie frowns.

Blue and yellow, dude – Banna! (*Almost hissing.*) 'Cos it's a beach house!

Howie That's . . . genius!

JJ Yer walking down the strand, gorgeous yellow sand 'tween your toes, taking the flags down, not a care in the world . . . I'm waving at yer from my stand. Real lifeguards, dude, that's what we are. Can ye see me waving, Howie?

Howie I can!

JJ Look how fecking brown I am.

Howie Ye are, dude!

JJ We both are. Fecking vigilant, dude. Nothing getting past us.

Howie Eagle-eyed.

JJ That's right, dude, we're eagle-eyed 'cos even though there's no rip-tide at Banna, we're vigilant and aware.

Ye see something, something not quite right, and what do ye do?

Howie Er . . .

JJ You blow ye whistle. Ye blow, Howie, and everything . . . stops. Like even the fecking waves stop and everyone looks at yer, 'cos you're the lifeguard, that's who you are. And if the lifeguard shoots the red flag up, you can't go into the water and nobody does go into the water. And when ye start to sprint all of a sudden, like lifeguards do, then they follow yer, 'cos everybody wants to be part of yer crowd, part of yer spectacle. Yer saving some dude's life, piece of fecking pish, Howie, everybody watching, everybody clapping. People asking to have their photograph taken with you. Girls trying to fuck you. Girls trying so hard to really fuck you . . .

Howie It's brilliant, JJ . . .

JJ Get on the lookout, Howie.

Howie climbs and settles into the seat, entranced.

You're on your stand, where are you?

Howie Er . . . I'm up here, JJ.

JJ You're high above the beach like a fecking bronze statue, you're raised up high, you're still as a fecking bronze, sun burning the back of your neck . . . Yer watching, yer not missing a trick, everything small, Howie, everything tiny. There yer are, and yer the big fellow, the big guy, yer the fecking main man. Howie, yer looking – (*Enunciating.*) – at the fecking bigger picture. Now do you still want to be a lifeguard at Banna, dude?

Howie Yes . . . You know I do! What will I do, JJ?

JJ Hold on so . . . (*A look to the sea.*) It looks calm enough now. We'll put up the green flag so.

He raises the green flag.

Just keep your head and look out for Brendan. Can you manage that?

Howie Course I can.

He looks to the left through his binoculars.

Clear.

He looks to the right.

Clear.

Brendan enters from the left, carrying his boots, a holdall and a clipboard.

Ah Jeezus! Brendan.

Brendan Lads, I'd say I surprised ye. I'd say I'm quite light on the old toes so. Were you surprised to see me, Howard? So I can tick that little box so. (*He ticks.*) Good afternoon, Howard.

Howie (*shocked*) Ger-goo . . .

Brendan (*making exaggerated facial expressions*) Put the tongue to the roof of the mouth, Howard. Now breathe down through the nostrils . . . Good after . . . Good afternoon . . . A lazy tongue doesn't have to mean a . . .? A lazy boy, Howard. (*Beat.*) Necessarily. Good afternoon, John-Joseph.

JJ nods.

Howie Ger . . . good afternoon, Mr McAllister.

Brendan Brendan. It's Brendan. Well now, come down now, Howard.

Howie comes down.

(*Smiling, looking about.*) I am pleasantly surprised. I'd say I was very pleasantly surprised. I'd say I could tick a few more of my little boxes here, all in the affirmative. (*Walking about. Nodding and ticking.*) I'd say . . . what's that smell?

JJ What smell, Brendan?

Brendan (*breathing in exaggeratedly*) Exactly. Exactly. I'd expect like, say, to smell like auld rubbish and aaauld seagull blood, but this smells, almost . . . like fresh air. You're doing very well so far. Very well indeed, lads. (*He ticks.*)

Howie *and* **JJ** Thanks, Brendan.

JJ Will I show you the logbooks, Brendan so? We have them all ready.

Brendan (*looking at his watch*) Well, now . . . I don't know. I have the Castlegrey boys to surprise too . . . I'd say the twins are in a tizz now, waiting on me. (*Beat.*) As it should be. I'll accept the offer of a cup of tea so.

JJ Howie . . . ?

Howie starts to make tea.

I'll show you the books so. They're all shipshape. Shall we? (*Gesturing to the hut.*)

Brendan All in good time.

He smiles. JJ and Howie stare nervously back. Brendan looks around and then sits and starts lacing his boots.

I'll go in for my swim later after I've made a full inspection between the flags. Then we'll test the authenticity of your descriptions. You have the green flag up. Were you in for a swim yerselfs?

Howie No.

JJ (*simultaneously*) Yes . . . Yes, we were . . . it's calm all right. That's right, isn't it, Howie?

Howie Right.

Brendan takes a packet of cigarettes from his pocket. JJ signals to Howie not to take one.

Brendan Fag?

JJ We don't smoke, Brendan.

Brendan ticks a box

Brendan Good. (*He gets up and then sits down again and lights a fag. Beat.*) You know this puts me in mind now of a day many summers ago now. Many summers ago. Perhaps you'll recall it, John-Joseph? You were in your prime then, I'd say. Walking down the road with yer wee entourage. All the girls hanging off yer. Do yer remember those days, John-Joseph?

JJ I do, Brendan.

Brendan Ye were there as well, Howard. Running after the man. I'd say you were about six . . . Off after him like the little puppy you were. Off for a day at the beach with your surfboards and yer girlfriends and yer cans. And for all I was in my own Peugeot and for all I was already on my way to my own office with my own private secretary and had already made a name for myself as a young councillor in the Planning Office, arbitrating boundary wars with farmers, a hard job, that's what my job was at the time . . . those farmers – (*Smiling, tight, stopping himself.*) Though I should not be boring ye with me unfinished business . . . (*Beat.*) I've upset myself now. (*Recovering.*) I saw ye all in my wing-mirror, a golden crowd ye were, all the girls laughing at yer jokes, John-Joseph, all the boys hanging off yer words. Do you recall that day, John-Joseph?

JJ Not that particular day, Brendan, no.

Brendan Just an ordinary day for you. But for me? I was already supporting the auld parents, God love them,

58

fetching and carrying for them, a heavy responsibility, and one I very gladly shoulder today, my own daddy in particular, he can be, well . . . very particular in his demands. Very – (*He chuckles without mirth.*) – *singular* in that respect. I was already supporting old Joan and though I had air conditioning in the Peugeot I started to sweat. What harm, thought I, if I just took a few hours off from the auld dry work? Had a bit of a swim, maybe ask ye for a loan of yer surfboard . . .

JJ Ye'd have been very welcome to it, Brendan.

Brendan Would I now? (*Pause.*) Ye don't remember that day, do ye?

JJ I don't, Brendan.

Brendan No matter. I have ye to thank though. I'd never have gotten interested in Leisure Services and Leisure Operatives if it wasn't for that day. Myself and old Joan now, we've had the great pleasure to be instrumental in building the Leisure Operatives of tomorrow. (*Getting up.*) Old Joan in particular with her after-school swimming club, the Little Fishes. The Dolphins. The Big Whalers. All the lads at the swimming pool doting on her. Absolutely doting . . . Add that to the Lingua courses we've tucked under our belts over the years on top of, on top of an exacting regime of the mind, a regiment of constant and restless self-improvement and anyone would see we have a full and productive life. The evenings pass like dreams.

JJ How is old Joan, Brendan? I meant to ask.

Brendan I'd not be breaking brother–sister confidentiality if I was to say she's on cloud fecking nine, John-Joseph.

JJ Say I was asking after her.

Brendan You can say that to herself on Saturday.

JJ I'm not . . . Saturday?

Brendan We're all off to see the aul' parents on Saturday. Joan wants to introduce ye?

JJ I think . . . I think there's been a . . . misunderstanding, Brendan.

Brendan Ah, there's no misunderstanding. There have been promises made and Joan, well . . . Whatever it is ye had, John-Joseph, well . . . (*He considers.*) You have it still. The birds from the trees. I haven't seen her like that now since the Brandon Hotel Christmas past. Ye've the candle lit in her. She's as giddy as a girl. It's a formal occasion, I'm afraid. Daddy is insisting and, well, it's a surprise, but old Joan she's bought a new outfit so you'll have to brush up. A suit and tie would be grand. Nothing fancy.

JJ I . . . I don't own a suit, Brendan.

Brendan Yer do, John-Joseph. Yer daddy's had one ordered specially.

JJ My daddy?

Brendan Now I can't be standing here gassing when there are boxes to be ticked and boxes to be crossed and paces to be put. We'll have a look at the logbooks so. (*He starts to flick through the logbooks. To Howie.*) Until I tell you to stop. Drop.

Howie drops to the sand and starts doing rapid press-ups.

Brendan (*to JJ*) Have you a shovel, John-Joseph?

JJ (*carefully*) Yes . . .

Brendan You might want to take a walk down the strand so. There's something washed in with the tide. An old farmer's dog, I think it is. Drowned.

JJ takes out his burial shovel.

JJ I'll take care of it, Brendan. (*He starts to leave. He gives a hard chuckle.*) Remember, Howie. Keep your head.

JJ exits. Brendan stands over Howie.

Brendan Ten.

Howie (*breathing hard*) It's seventeen, Brendan . . .

Brendan Ten. Those first ones don't count. One arm now.

Howie tries. And fails.

Never mind that now. That was just a joke I'm playing on you. I've only seen that done on telly.

Howie (*getting up*) Have I passed, Brendan?

Brendan Well . . .

Howie Have I passed, sir?

Brendan Hmm. I would not be breaking Councillor and Inspector confidentiality if I was to say I have a few boxes to tick right enough. There's room for improvement, mind. Room I'd say for vast improvements, but old Joan has a soft spot for her wee Dolphin man, as she calls you, she said I wasn't to be too hard on ye.

Howie Will you say I was asking after her. Just to say hello, like? Not to be going out or anything like that.

Brendan I will, Howard.

Howie She was always very kind to me, old Joan. When me mammy got sick like . . .

Brendan I don't want to hear your orphan shite now, Howard.

Howie Yes, sir, it's just . . .

Brendan (*lighting a cigarette*) There are worse things then being an orphan, Howard.

Howie Are there, Brendan? I mean, there are? Like what?

Brendan Like – (*as he exhales*) – not being an orphan, Howard. What is the first thing you do with a drowning victim?

Howie Eh?

Brendan What is the first thing you do with a drowning victim?

Howie You er . . .

Brendan You have ten seconds.

Howie (*thinking*) You check the airways for debris!

Brendan (*ticks*) Good. And you . . .?

Howie Clear the airways, sir.

Brendan You're a lifeguard on a deserted, somewhat unpopular beach in Ireland. What are you?

Howie A lifeguard, Brendan.

Brendan A-ware, Howard. You're vig-il-lant. And why are you so watchful, Howard?

Howie (*thinking hard*) I'm a . . . I'm an orphan, Brendan?

Brendan (*beat*) What are you?

Howie I'm a . . . a lifeguard, Brendan?

Brendan Correct. And a lifeguard has to be . . .? Vigilant at all times. You must have eyes like lasers, boy.

Howie straightens up and starts to check the horizon.

You must be constantly raking the horizon Your boss arrives to do a little spot-check. He's an important man right enough, bearing the full authority of the local council. Do you let the importance of this visitor distract you from your . . . I was going to say job, Howard . . . but saving lives is a vocation. So? You do not. Do you stop raking the horizon, Howard? You do not. Let me put it another way, Howard . . . Would you leave a baby alone in a bath?

Howie I . . . er, a baby, Brendan? Er . . . (*Guessing.*) No. No, I would not let a baby alone in a bath.

Brendan Gooood. (*He ticks.*)

Howie Will you be going in for a swim now, Brendan? The water's warm, you know. (*Laughs.*) I . . . I plugged in the central heating for you myself. I'd say it is a beautiful temperature now.

Brendan I might. I might. There's a new stroke I've developed. It'd defy a rip-tide, I have every confidence. Half a front crawl and a bit of this. (*He demonstrates.*)

Howie That looks . . . useful.

Brendan It's revolutionary, boy.

Howie Show us it again.

   Brendan demonstrates, Howie copies.

That's genius!

Brendan It's ergonomic. It shaves vital seconds off my own front crawl. On a surfboard I'd say it was lethal.

Howie I'd say it was the best stroke I've ever seen.

Brendan Thanks.

Howie I'd say it was the most advanced stroke I've seen in a long time.

Brendan That's enough, Howard.

Howie I'd say a whole team of Olympic swimmers couldn't do it fecking better.

Brendan That'll do, Howard.

Howie I'd say you could cut the sea in two with a stroke that deadly . . .

Brendan That's enough now, Howard.

Howie (*beat*) I was only after saying. With a stroke like that . . .

Brendan Shut up.

Howie (*beat*) It's just I'm nervous, Brendan.

Brendan I know, Howard. You've nothing to be nervous about. Your place is secured. Sign here now.

Brendan holds out the clipboard. Howie signs.

Howie I passed?

Brendan (*enjoying himself*) Banna would be a different story now, there's different tests for Banna Strand entirely, but wisely, perhaps unwisely, who can say, knowing your own strengths and weaknesses as ye do – (*Beat.*) – you did not apply . . . Ye worked it out between yer with no hard feelings on either side.

Howie Huh?

Brendan That's grand and as it should be. But you passed here today so . . .

Howie I passed?

Brendan Of course you passed. Who else would I get to work here? You have the rest of the summer paid for. Tell himself to be on guard so while I do the twins. Expect me when you least expect me. (*He exits.*)

Howie (*dancing about*) I PASSED I PASSED I PASSED I PASSED. I . . .

64

Suddenly, he freezes. Pause. He makes a bee-line for the hut and starts to search amongst the detritus outside. JJ enters, dropping the shovel onto the sand.

JJ How was it? (*Pause.*) I said how was it, dude? What did he ask you?

Howie I'd say it went well.

JJ starts warm-up exercises.

JJ I'm ready. I'd say I'm as ready as I'll ever be. What questions did he ask yer?

Howie Basic life-saving procedures, dude. You know.

JJ Like what?

Howie About drowning and suchlike.

JJ Like fecking what, Howie?

Howie Like what was on pages 110 to 115, JJ.

JJ Eh?

Howie The ones I wiped my arse with. Like how to save someone from drowning.

JJ Have you fecking knocked ye head?

Howie Hang on a second now . . . I'm just looking for . . .

Howie disappears inside the hut. Sounds of rummage.

JJ Don't be going messing, Howie. It's fecking perfect in there. Don't touch any fecking thing.

No answer.

Come down from there, Howie, and talk some fecking sense. (*To himself.*) If ye fecking can.

Howie (*offstage*) I haven't found it yet.

JJ What?

Howie (*offstage*) My application.

JJ What? . . . Come out now, wee eejit-dude.

He goes to the doorway and backs out. Howie emerges, aiming the rifle at JJ.

Howie Who's the eejit-dude now?

JJ Dude. There's no time for one of yer fecking blowouts. Fecking Brendan is . . .

Howie I don't fecking care about Brendan! (*He backs JJ around the hut.*) You're a fecking liar. That's all ye are. Ye fecking lie about everything.

Pause.

JJ I wasn't lying about Banna, dude . . .

Howie I fecking know you were, dude-cunt! (*Pause.*) Ye didn't even send in my application did ye, JJ?

JJ No.

Howie Were ye just going to leave me here? With them?

JJ I thought maybe Tommy Frank . . .

Howie Scratchy?

JJ There was only one vacancy at Banna, Howie.

Howie And you think you're the one to get it, do you?

JJ I earnt it!

Howie I fecking earned it! (*He lifts the rifle, shaking, and aims.*)

JJ Ye wouldn't fecking dare.

Howie cocks the gun.

(*Pointing.*) What's that?

Howie looks. JJ disarms him.

66

Yer finished here. Ye might as well get your wheels and skate off to Mrs Simmonds. She'll have your dinner waiting for you in the cat bowl.

Howie Feck off.

Howie throws sand at JJ. JJ throws sand at Howie.

JJ Feck off yourself.

Howie Why don't ye tell me one of your great surfing stories to pass the fecking time, dude? Why don't you . . . why don't you tell me about the time you saved the millionaire's daughter with your special kiss of life technique, the one you fecking miraculously forgot with Grace, and the fat man and the ol' lady tramp, and how ye only got a handshake but ye didn't mind because life doesn't have a price, am I quoting you fecking correctly? And why don't ye tell me about how the air smelt of like coconut oil and Coppertone Factor fecking One and about yer fecking six pack . . . and how you robbed your buddy-dudes . . .

JJ (*shovelling sand at Howie*) I did not rob my buddy-dudes.

Howie Why not? You fecking robbed me. Ye bet my inheritance on a fecking hobbled horse . . .

JJ You wanted to bet it.

Howie I was *fifteen years old*. All the time I'm giving and I'm giving and yer taking. Yer taking my wages. Yer telling me stories, I'm fecking believing ye for five fecking years. Soaking it up. Everyone saying, don't believe that lying cunt John-Joseph McKeown. Me defending yer. Eating scraps for five fecking years. Burying people just because ye say so. Thinking we were buds. Thinking we were dudes. Saving for a flat. Dreaming about Banna. If I'd known you were a lying little fat fecking robber . . .

JJ You knew! You've fecking always known.

Howie (*faintly*) . . . What?

JJ (*mimicking*) 'What?' (*Punching Howie on the arm.*) Did ye think I hung out with you because I . . . I wanted to? You got to hang out with me. I'm JJ. I'm John-Joseph McKeown. You got to sit next to me. You're only wearing that jacket because of me. You'd be up to your arse in giblets all year round if it wasn't for me. So I fecking taxed yer. I had to put up with a stinky shitey wee moron-dude. I should have taxed your arse a lot more.

Howie (*shakily*) Feck off.

JJ No, you feck off. So I told a few stories. At least it was better than your fecking cancer stories and bleating about yer fecking dead relatives, yer contagious little . . .

Howie My own mammy . . .

JJ Your mammy, your fecking daddy . . .

Howie My sister Majella . . .

JJ How could I forget your sister fecking Majella . . .

Howie (*bawling*) My three aunts . . .

Starting to circle each other . . .

JJ Bleating and fecking going on. Just because ye whole fecking family drops fecking dead ye think you can go on and on boring me fecking arse . . . Playing the orphan. Poor fecking Howie. But I know you, Dowd. I know you. (*He points.*) You Eat Sweeties From A Dead Man's Togs.

Howie runs with a roar at JJ. JJ does his feint, but Howie keeps on coming. JJ backs against the open door of the hut. We hear the clang of metal as Howie picks up the hammer from a bucket and advances on him.

(*Frightened.*) H-howie, hold on now. Keep your head.

Howie You're the one who's going to lose their fecking head.

The buried Girl suddenly appears sheathed in wet sand, still wearing her veil. She looks ghastly. JJ raises a finger and gives a horrified squeal.

JJ (*barely a gasp*) Howie . . . 'tis the dead thing.

Howie doesn't turn round.

Howie Think I'm going to fall for that? Who is it? The fat man wanting his fecking lunch? (*Over his shoulder.*) I'll have something for ye in a minute.

He raises the hammer.

Girl Ow, ow, ow . . .

Howie freezes. He turns slowly round. The hammer drops from his hand. The two men stare at the veiled Girl, who sways in front of them. A long beat. She steadies herself and raises her veil. Her face is bloody.

Am I dead? Is this being dead?

Howie is speechless.

Girl (*to Howie*) I asked you a fecking civilised question.

Howie You're . . . alive?

Girl Feck it. Who saved me?

Howie (*hoarse*) He did.

JJ He . . .

Girl (*beat*) Did I fecking ask to be saved? Was I fecking waving? Did you see a fecking sign round my neck saying SAVE ME? What gives you the fecking holy right to . . .

Howie We're . . . we're lifeguards. It's our job.

Girl I asked you a civilised question. (*She gives her head a shake.*)

Howie JJ . . .

Girl I'm talking! (*Very fast, a babble.*) I've been incarcerated . . . incarcerated for eight fecking years. I was in . . . I . . . the Priory Home for Wayward Girls! I thought it was a kind of holiday camp. I was . . . I was . . . I was in Sister Angelica's office. I don't know how I got in there because nobody in the community is allowed in there but I had . . . privileges, that's right, as the longest-serving inmate. I had my hands in the filing cabinet and I found my file. My own file in the filing cabinet . . . and I was amazed to find I'd been incarcerated for eight fecking years. They gave me pills. Red ones. And green ones. I pretended to swallow with my cake but I did not. I was at the gates and it was so easy to get out. I could have just gone years ago. I stepped out. And I walked and I remembered what made me so unhappy in the first place. I remembered.

She washes the blood from her face with JJ's shaving water.

JJ (*softly*) Ah Jesus!

Girl And I saw myself waiting for him in me white dress, me flowers in me hair. Waiting like the fecking fool.

JJ Feck feck feck . . .

Girl And him, my fecking fiancé not being where he ought to have been, where he promised he would be. 'It's just a loan,' said he. 'I'll be back,' said he.

Howie JJ?

Girl Off to California with our honeymoon fund. He promised to marry me.

Howie JJ, is that . . . ?

JJ Ah feck . . . it's whatshername.

Girl My name is Ursula O'Sullivan!

She looks down at her bloody dress.

Ursula I've blood . . . on . . . my . . . wedding . . . gown. 'Tis the fecking giddy limit.

JJ Ursula, I can explain.

Ursula And that's what started all this . . . this Orphelia shite in the first place. Eight years of my fecking life.

Howie I think . . . I think she's really angry, JJ.

JJ You think?

Ursula (*throwing stones at Howie*) Sick of waiting for him. Wanting to kill myself. Walking under the cold . . .

Howie Ouch! Ouch! Ouch! I didn't do nutting to you, Grace. I mean Ursula.

Ursula Didn't ye bury me alive and wrap my head in a stinking towel?

Howie No.

Ursula Didn't ye bury me alive with an auld stinky towel?

Howie Okay, yes. But he made me.

Ursula And didn't you talk to me and talk to me and talk to me till I wanted to asphyxiate?

Howie I was just . . . I was just – (*Starting to bawl.*) – trying to be nice.

JJ Leave him alone, Ursula. He's an orphan.

Howie Thanks, dude.

Ursula (*turning on him*) And you . . . You . . . Did you think I didn't recognise yer? Do you think I don't know yer, John-Joseph McKeown? Have a fecking diamond.

She throws a rock at him. JJ dodges it.

JJ I . . . I can only apologise, Ursula. It wasn't . . . personal. But if it's any consolation now, I don't think . . . I don't think we would have been happy.

Ursula takes a note out of her bodice.

Ursula Read it. (*Beat.*) 'Tis laminated.

JJ There's no need . . .

Ursula Read it!

JJ reads it.

Out loud.

JJ (*reading very quickly*) 'Now you will feel no rain, for each of you will be the . . . the tent for each other. Two people but there is only one life before you. May beauty surround you both in the journey ahead through all the years. May happiness be your companion and your days together be good and long upon the earth.'

Ursula Down on your knee so. (*Beat.*) Kneel.

JJ gets down on one knee.

Say it?

JJ (*coughing*) Will you marry me, Ursula O'Sullivan?

Ursula stares at him.

Ursula (*beat*) No! You've got to be . . . I'd rather die. Look at the fecking state of ye. Who'd have ye? (*To herself, wondering.*) 'Tis gone. 'Tis gone . . . I've nothing now.

JJ You've had a bad bump on the head, Ursula. I think you should see a . . .

Ursula Garda?

JJ There's no need for that.

Howie (*a whimper*) JJ?

Ursula Attempted murder. Burying alive betwixt dog and cow. Looting of my poor deluded corpse. I think there is indeed a need for a garda. I feel so . . . ah . . .

She puts her hands in her hair, holding a huge bunch of it.

What the feck's this?

Howie JJ? Is she going to call a garda, JJ? Is she?

Ursula stares at them, coming to a decision.

Ursula Feck yers . . . I'm done. (*She walks away into the sea.*) Tell Daddy I said ta-ta.

She exits.

Howie JJ? Is she . . . ?

JJ (*binoculars*) She fecking is! Feck . . . feck!

They start to exit, tearing off their clothes.

Quick black. Staying in the darkness – the shrill of a whistle.

TWO

JJ and Howie are soaking wet and are life-saving Ursula crisply and efficiently. Brendan is watching and ticking little boxes on his clipboard.

Brendan Well done, lads. Now . . . now . . . put her in the recovery position any . . .

All Sea water should flow out.

Brendan Well done, lads.

Ursula coughs mightily and lies panting. JJ gets to work wrapping a bandage round her head.

I'd say that was the best sea rescue I've seen in a . . . well, I've seen in a long time. It was almost textbook stuff.

Howie stands and beams.

The way you, John-Joseph, swam in with the surfboard, without panic but with due precision, taking a good few knocks and bruises from the rocks therein.

JJ I was only doing my job, Brendan.

Brendan And you, Howard, the way you dragged her back in by the hair and took your turn at the old mouth-to-mouth like your own life depended on it.

Howie I was just doing my job, Brendan.

Brendan It was cracking stuff. I'm only glad I was alerted by your shout and whistle and had the good fortune to witness the whole rescue from start to finish. How is the patient?

JJ She's . . . she has a . . . couple of bad head wounds, Brendan, but I think, I think she's going to be okay.

Ursula moans. JJ quietens her.

Shh now, don't try to speak.

Brendan has a good look at her.

Brendan I'd say you're being a tad on the generous side with the bandages there, John-Joseph. You've nearly her mouth taped shut.

JJ Have I?

Brendan goes to loosen the bandages.

Brendan Is that better?

Ursula Urhhhh!

Brendan Isn't that . . . isn't this Teddy O'Sullivan's girl, John-Joseph? . . . The one up at the Wayward? 'Tis Ursula . . .

JJ Is it?

Howie Is it?

Ursula pats about for a rock.

Brendan (*tending to her*) Ursula, dear girl, can you speak? Can you speak? I think she's trying to say something. How could you not recognise your own ex-fiancée, John-Joseph?

JJ (*babbling*) I . . . I don't know. It's been eight . . . a long time, Brendan. And I think she had like a little bob. And she wasn't like all covered in blood and scabs and puke . . . It was a long time ago . . . and I don't think I fecking hardly knew her. And she was about fecking three stone lighter . . .

Brendan Fair enough. I'd say she's put on the beef all right. Those nuns – (*Shaking his head.*) They're all cake and barbiturates. (*He takes hold of her. He gestures at Howie's red blanky.*) Give's that rag here, Howie.

Howie hesitates, then hands it over. Brendan puts it over the Girl's shoulders. She slumps against him.

Well, I won't be breaking councillor confidentiality if I was to say you've done yourself a big favour here, John-Joseph. A big favour. I'd say Teddy O'Sullivan will be very grateful to you from now on for saving his daughter instead of hating your guts for destroying her in the first place and wishing you to hell and barracking myself to promote one of the Castlegrey twins above ye. A very big favour.

Ursula starts to mumble.

What's that now?

Ursula (*delirious, happy, eyes closed*) 'Tis done. I'm at rest now, that's where I am. When I open my eyes 'twill be

75

like . . . like a . . . beautiful garden bathed in sunshine . . .
Holy sunshine. Beauty will surround me in the beautiful
garden . . .

Brendan (*overlapping*) How's that? Talk sense now.

Howie I think she's still like a mental eejit, JJ.

Brendan Shush now . . .

Ursula It will be too beautiful to gaze upon. That's the
only worry I have. My eyes might not be wide enough for
the beautiful sight. I'll open them so. (*She opens her eyes
and looks about her. Her happy smile fades.*) This is not a
beautiful garden.

Brendan No. Well, 'tis no Banna. Not by a long chalk.
Am I right, lads?

JJ *and* **Howie** Ye are, Brendan. / Yes Brendan.

Ursula stares at them with some intelligence. Beat.

Howie (*faintly*) Dude . . .

She turns to Brendan.

Ursula Am I dead?

Brendan What? (*Chuckling, a wink at JJ and Howie.*)
Are ye dead? (*Beat, looking at her.*) Course ye are, ye wee
dafty. Course ye are. We all are, aren't we, lads?

JJ *and* **Howie** Yes, Brendan.

Brendan helps Ursula up.

Brendan Shush now and we'll pop up to Heaven, shall
we's, and get Annie to ring for a nun. We'll get you
medicated so. Will that do you? I'd say it would. (*As they
exit, agreeing.*) 'Tis a pretty rock, yes.

*Pause. JJ lights a cigarette. A beat. He gives the packet
to Howie. They smoke. Pause.*

Howie I bet yer were never even near California or a fecking beach, were you, dude?

JJ I was.

Pause.

Howie Were you ever a lifeguard in California, JJ?

JJ Yes.

Howie Were ye ever a lifeguard in California, JJ?

JJ No.

Pause.

Howie Can ye even speak Russian?

JJ (*exhaling*) Not really, no.

Howie What did you do in California so?

JJ I worked in a burger bar. It was on the beachfront, though. I could see them through this little window. I could see the lifeguards on their stands. I could see those dudes all day long. (*Beat.*) Ye should have seen them, Howie, like gods . . .

Howie I'd say ye still want that job at Banna, dude.

JJ turns away. Howie comes up close to him.

Have the job at Banna, dude.

JJ (*beat*) . . . What?

Howie I don't think I could do Banna on my own. I'd kack myself. I'll not stand in your way. And . . . and someone has to look after them.

JJ (*stunned*) But . . . feck, dude. I don't know what to say. Feck! Feck! Thanks, dude.

JJ goes to embrace Howie. Second thoughts. He wrings Howie's hand instead with real emotion.

Howie Dudes!

JJ Dudes!

Howie We saved her after all, didn't we, dude?

JJ We did.

Howie We saved her the second time and we saved her the first time. Our fecking efforts there were not wasted.

JJ That's a way of looking at it, dude.

Howie We were like proper lifeguards, weren't we, dude?

JJ We were, dude.

Howie Fecking . . . eagle-eyed . . .

JJ Nothing getting passed us . . .

Howie Vig-il-ant and . . .

JJ A-ware.

Brendan walks in behind them holding his clipboard. With a glance at the shovel.

Brendan So, ye buried the bitch?

Howie and JJ turn and gape at him.

JJ (*realising*) The dog. We buried the farmer's dog. We have that taken care of, haven't we, Howie?

Howie nods. Brendan smiles at them a little fixedly.

Brendan (*beat*) Lads, well, it's been a long day now and I have – (*He ticks*) – a few boxes to finish off before my swim – all, I add, in the affirmative. I've had a looksy through the logbooks and – so far – they are in order though they are . . .

Howie Succinct?

Brendan Good, Howard. Succinct could be applied to the brief descriptions therein. But, in general, in general,

I'd say I was impressed with yer teamwork today. I was up at Castlegrey surprising the twins and I found them at each other's t'roats . . . at each other's t'roats. 'Tis not easy being a Leisure Operative in the modern world, it's not all 'staring' as some councillors suppose. Now, what have I forgotten? I've forgotten something, now what is it?

JJ Uh . . . the post at Banna, Brendan. Perhaps you have some news for me?

Brendan Dear me, what am I like? Keeping you on tenterhooks when that was not my intention, but with all the excitement over the rescue, well, I'm sure you'll forgive the tardiness in my response to yon application. Which I might add was excellently written and presented. 'Retrieved from their relieved parents', I particularly liked that. I like a little – (*Beat.*) – assonance. Your daddy can be very proud of you for that alone. (*Smiles.*) I'd say I'm favourably impressed, lads . . .

Beat. Brendan advances suddenly and shakes Howie's hand.

Brendan Ye have the season secured so. Well done, Howard.

Howie Thanks, Brendan.

Brendan Congratulations to yor both. If you'd put your squiggle here, John-Joseph – (*Holding out the clipboard.*) We can dispense with the formalities.

JJ signs. Brendan shakes JJ's hand. A double handshake.

I'd say the best man won. I'll change into my togs so. It's the green flag is it, JJ, does that still hold?

JJ nods.

Good man.

He goes into the hut. Howie turns to JJ.

Howie Dude, ye have it in the bag so. He's fecking going to give you Banna!

JJ (*smiling, slightly stunned*) I think he is. Feck.

Howie Feck's sake, we've done it. I'll visit every weekend!

JJ (*beat*) Great.

Howie We're going to Banna for our summer holidays!

JJ We are.

Howie We could have those ham salads. And fags. Fags coming out of our ears.

JJ Right.

Howie We could have barbecues. And sleepovers in the state-of-the-art caravan.

JJ We will.

Howie It's all thanks to me, isn't it, dude?

JJ (*beat*) 'Tis.

Brendan comes out, dressed in a long towelling dressing gown with a black armband. Sandals. He takes off his glasses and puts them in his robe.

Brendan I don't need these fellows quite as much as I did in the old days. Have ye heard of laser therapy? It's revolutionised the eye industry. (*Pause.*) Now this . . . this reminds me of that occasion I mentioned earlier, John-Joseph. I wonder if you recall it now?

JJ About Banna, Brendan? You were going to . . .

Brendan That day I was telling you about earlier. When I saw you all off for a swim, oh, many moons ago now.

A golden day. The sun was shining through the sun roof . . . The surf was high. I decided I'd have a little swim myself, a little break from my myriad dry old responsibilities. So I stripped off on the beach. You lads were in a big gang, laughing and joking. (*Smiling to himself.*) Can you recall any of those jokes now, John-Joseph?

JJ (*slowly recalling*) I think . . . that was just . . . high spirits, Brendan. It was only teasing.

Brendan Of course it was! I never thought any more about it. (*Beat.*) Not a thought more. Well, as I said, I thought no more about it. Till the tragic accident with young Sean and Jimmy. Life is short, I said to myself. Life is so short and here am I nearly . . . well, getting on in life, and I haven't even had my summer yet.

JJ About Banna, Brendan . . .

Brendan The post is taken, JJ.

JJ (*shocked*) You've given it to one of the fecking twins so! I fecking knew . . .

Brendan No.

Brendan drops his robe revealing a smart wet-suit. Pause. Howie lets out an incredulous snort of laughter. JJ is staggered. Brendan pulls up the hood of the wet-suit and pulls goggles onto his forehead. He picks up a surfboard and prepares to leave.

JJ You . . .

Brendan Congratulations to you both for passing the inspection so. I won't be breaking councillor confidentiality when I say the pair of ye have made improvements beyond and above my expectations, which were not high to start with. Ye've staved off a hard decision with yer impressive deep clean and yer impressive rescue of a councillor's daughter. Who knows what the future will hold. I'd say we'll keep the beach open so a good few years yet. I'll see you on Saturday so, John-Joseph, about eight.

JJ You must be joking. I wouldn't touch old Joan now with a . . .

Brendan turns. A formidable presence.

Brendan I'd say about eight, John-Joseph.

JJ Yes, Brendan.

Brendan Climb into the bucket seat, then, Howie, keep an eye on me. (*Chuckling.*) I may want rescuing.

Howie I will, Brendan.

Howie starts to climb. Brendan turns back.

Brendan (*smiling, quizzical*) Aren't ye a pair of dark horses?

JJ (*faintly*) What?

Brendan Are you trying to earn a car park?

JJ I'm not following you, Brendan.

Brendan (*taking off his sandals*) Ye've had visitors. Don't be shy now, admit it. Yer visitors left personal property behind in the shape of a watch and sundry other items. A pen, a brooch . . . 'Twas all in a box in the hut. Ye forgot to log said items as lost property. I needn't remind ye all lost property must be logged, as well ye know, but as the day is nearly done I took the liberty of ticking a few of the boxes myself. 'Tis a fine watch, an expensive one. Whoever 'PT' is he'll be eternally thankful for its return. And Joan will be able to help you out with the silver brooch. She'll turn detective for yer. We'll find them all homes so, ye can be sure of that. I'm impressed, lads. Where there's one visitor, two will come. Where there's three, yer building yer own holiday crowd. We should have offered an incentive a long time ago. I'll go in for my swim so. (*Pulling his goggles down.*) Watch me now.

He exits. We hear the lonely wind and the seagulls cawing. JJ and Howie stand watch.

Howie Dude, they'll come looking . . .

JJ I know, dude.

Pause.

Howie The current might take him.

They watch. Their postures sag as the current doesn't take Brendan. Howie resignedly pulls out his rifle and climbs up into the bucket seat. He aims the gun, tracking Brendan in his sights. JJ has his shovel ready.

They'll send another inspector.

JJ I know, dude.

Blackout.

The End.